lies
about
my family

University of Massachusetts Press   Amherst and Boston

Amy Hoffman

# lies
## about
# my family

ISBN 978-1-55849-003-0 paperback
ISBN 978-1-55849-002-3 hardcover

Designed by Sally Nichols
Set in Chapparel Pro
Printed and bound by Thomson-Shore, Inc.


Library of Congress Cataloging-in-Publication Data

Hoffman, Amy, author.
Lies about my family : a memoir / Amy Hoffman.
pages cm
ISBN 978-1-62534-003-0 (pbk. : alk. paper) — ISBN 978-1-62534-002-3
(hardcover : alk. paper) 1. Hoffman, Amy. 2. Rutherford (N.J.)—Biography.
3. Jews—New Jersey—Rutherford—Biography. 4. Jewish lesbians—Biography.
5. Hoffman family. I. Title.
F144.R9H64 2013
974.9′2104092—dc23
[B]
2012050133


British Library Cataloguing-in-Publication Data
A catalogue record for this book is available
from the British Library.

to my parents

Here it is, my story—yours is probably different. You write yours.

—Aunt Norma

# contents

# — GINSBURGS —

[Simplified]

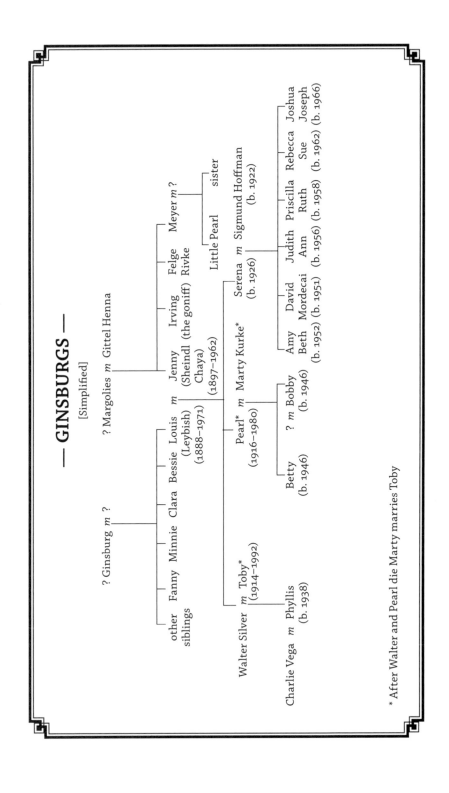

? Margolies *m* Gittel Henna

? Ginsburg *m* ?

other siblings — Fanny — Minnie — Clara — Bessie — Louis (Leybish) (1888–1971) *m* Jenny (Sheindl Chaya) (1897–1962) — Irving (the goniff) — Felge Rivke — Meyer *m* ? — sister

Little Pearl

Walter Silver *m* Toby* (1914–1992)

Pearl* (1916–1980) *m* Marty Kurke*

Serena (b. 1926) *m* Sigmund Hoffman (b. 1922)

Charlie Vega *m* Phyllis (b. 1938)

Betty (b. 1946)

? *m* Bobby (b. 1946)

Amy Beth (b. 1952)
David Mordecai (b. 1951)
Judith Ann (b. 1956)
Priscilla Ruth (b. 1958)
Rebecca Sue (b. 1962)
Joshua Joseph (b. 1966)

* After Walter and Pearl die Marty marries Toby

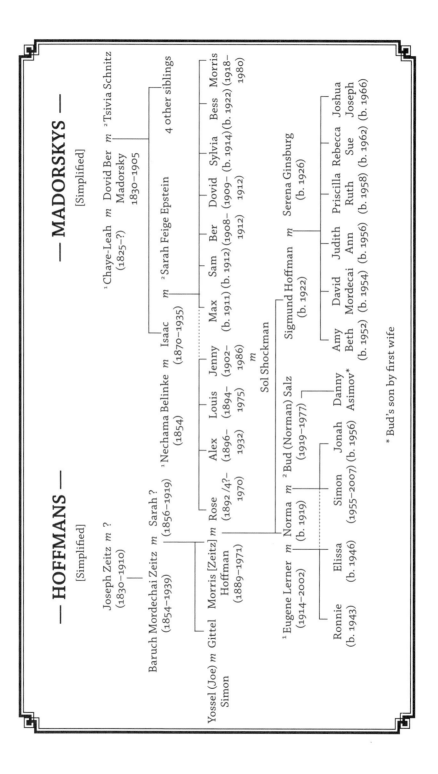

— HOFFMANS —

[Simplified]

Joseph Zeitz *m* ?
(1830–1910)

Baruch Mordechai Zeitz *m* Sarah ?
(1854–1939)                    (1856–1919)

Yossel (Joe) *m* Gittel  Morris [Zeitz] *m* Rose
Simon                    Hoffman         (1892/4?–
                         (1889–1971)     1970)

¹ Eugene Lerner *m* Norma *m* ² Bud (Norman) Salz
(1914–2002)        (b. 1919)        (1919–1977)

Ronnie          Elissa          Simon          Jonah          Danny
(b. 1943)       (b. 1946)       (1955–2007)    (b. 1956)      Asimov*

— MADORSKYS —

[Simplified]

¹ Chaye-Leah  *m*  Dovid Ber  *m*  ² Tsivia Schnitz
(1825–?)            Madorsky
                    1830–1905

                    4 other siblings

                    *m*  ² Sarah Feige Epstein

¹ Nechama Belinke  *m*  Isaac
(1854)                  (1870–1935)

Alex          Louis          Jenny          Max          Sam   Ber   Dovid   Sylvia   Bess   Morris
(1896–        (1894–         (1902–         (b. 1911)    (b. 1912) (1908– (1909–  (b. 1914) (b. 1922) (1918–
1932)         1975)          1986)                                 1912)  1912)                      1980)

                             *m*
                             Sol Shockman

Sigmund Hoffman  *m*  Serena Ginsburg
(b. 1922)             (b. 1926)

Amy          David      Judith    Priscilla   Rebecca   Joshua
Beth         Mordecai   Ann       Ruth        Sue       Joseph
(b. 1952)    (b. 1954)  (b. 1956) (b. 1958)   (b. 1962) (b. 1966)

* Bud's son by first wife

lies
about
my family

## spinning

**Hair.**  In response to an often-debated question about human nature: yes, people can change. Sometimes it may take a while. At eighty, musing about my sexual preference, my mother said, "I used to be so upset about it. Now I can't even remember why."

And just to be clear, she was not lamenting the forgetfulness of old age. Both of my parents' memories are as good as they ever were, *keynehora,* knock on wood. My myopic father's recall is as sharp as a hawk's eye—he can retrieve the name of seemingly everyone he's ever met, the date on which he met them, and their telephone number—while my mother's is blurred, as it's been throughout her life, by a pink cloud that generally allows through only the pleasant and the good.

Her admission touched me deeply, scattering in an instant years of isolation and hard feeling. There had been a period, an era, a great eon—from my mid-twenties to my early forties—when she and my father didn't talk about me. Jewish parents like to *kvell,* to take pleasure in their children's accomplishments, so much so that Yiddish has this special word for it—but with me, what was there to *kvell* about? That I'd edited a radical gay newspaper and then joined a collective press known for publishing the works of Noam Chomsky? That I'd shacked up with a woman with an asymmetrical haircut, and my best friend Richard was an immensely tall, obtrusive gay man with a booming voice? My life was a secret they kept.

I know this because during that period, whenever I attended a family event, someone would inevitably exclaim, "Amy! You cut your hair!"

But I'd cut my hair years before.

Throughout junior high and high school I had worn fat shiny braids that ended below my waist. When I was young, my mother used to brush and braid my hair each morning, although of course as I got older I did that myself.

Then, during the summer of my sophomore year of college, I was sharing a house with a bunch of other girls, one of whom was a feminist who insisted we call ourselves *women,* not *girls.* (I met a guy one afternoon, to whom I mentioned the *women* I lived with, and he said, "So does that make me a *man*?" and I thought, No, it doesn't.) The weather that summer was disgustingly hot, sticky and unrelenting, especially in the attic, which was my room, and my hair was so crazy thick and tangled that it would make a person sweat just to look at it. My feminist roommate came home one evening wearing a short, practical bob, and it looked so refreshing, I insisted she cut my hair, too. She started by slicing off my braids. Then, she hesitated.

"Keep going," I encouraged her, and she hacked away. The next day we all got into her car and drove to the Jersey Shore, and when the wind blew off the ocean, I felt as though I was wearing a funny little cap on my head.

The haircut was an impulse that for all my bravado I occasionally regretted. I missed the familiar weight of my hair on my shoulders and the ritual of braiding it each morning. The little decision: one today, or two? My hair had been my defining characteristic—if you'd been asked to describe me, you would have started with it. It made me beautiful. Old ladies, their own hair thin and blue—total strangers—would regularly stop me on the street and admonish me: "Never cut your hair. I had hair like that when I was a girl." Playfully, they'd tug on a braid.

But I wanted to be known and loved for my accomplishments, and how much does having long hair really say about a person? It's not as though growing hair is such a fabulous skill; it just happens, as you go about your business. As you're sleeping. A corpse can grow hair.

After the haircut my roommate had handed me my braids, and I saved them intact in a shoebox, because I thought my mother might want them—and in fact, she did. She kept them for years. Then at one point she came across them as she was cleaning out the attic, and the next time I visited she gave them back to me, as she often does with the random mementos that she turns up doing her chores. Not that she's much of a saver, but certain things tend to hang around—old report cards, baby pictures. Usually I just accept whatever it is and then when I get home, stick it in a drawer and forget about it, but the braids were creepy—dried out and faded. She insisted, though. Perhaps, she suggested, they were worth something: "They could be made into a wig."

"They've been in the attic for thirty years!" I said.

"Your old braids!" she said nostalgically, holding out the shoebox.

"Okay, okay, Ma." I took it from her and threw it into the back seat of the car. When I got home, I immediately tossed it into the trash can at the side of the house, not even carrying it upstairs to my apartment with the rest of my stuff.

Over the years, our family friends and relatives saw me with short hair on many occasions. But each time they were newly baffled by it, as though my life were held in suspension at that moment just before the scissors, my adolescent self sitting on a kitchen chair, a bath towel around my shoulders. They didn't ask me about myself, about where I was working, where I was living and with whom. They didn't bother to brag about the graduate degrees, the wealth, or the weddings of their kids, my

cousins and contemporaries. That was because of my parents'
silence, which had marked off me and my doings as forbidden
territory.

"As long as you're happy, darling," my mother had said when
I came out to her, and I'm sure she believed she meant it. I was
twenty-five. I invited her to go for a walk, and we ended up at
a muddy duck pond, staring into the cattails as I uttered the
word: *gay*. I had never called myself that before; my friends and
I always said *lesbian* or *dyke*, but somehow those words seemed
too graphic to use with my mother. I told her I was in love with
a woman—Cynthia. *Goddess of the moon*, I would add, to myself,
when I said her name. She was a high school English teacher.

I should have left it at *gay*. Giving my mother such specific
information was a mistake, since it enabled her to believe it
was something in Cynthia, not me, that had given rise to my
lesbian fad, and that once she was out of the picture, it would
end, and my mother could settle back into wondering whom I
would marry and when our babies would come. So for a time
she humored me, although she couldn't help occasionally sighing after my high-school boyfriend, who had become a rabbi
and married a woman named Amy. My parallel life. They have
three lovely children.

With my father, I never actually had the coming out conversation; it was just understood that anything my mother knew,
he knew also.

The next time I visited, I brought them books—*Now That You
Know; Sappho Was a Right-On Woman*. Our house was always
full of books, of all kinds—from my mother's English-major,
Modern Library classics and *The Interpretation of Dreams* in the
living room bookcase (which as a beginning reader I had thought
my parents must have bought because the author's name was
Sigmund, the same as my father's) to the paperback of *Fanny
Hill* in my parents' night-table—but the ones I gave them disappeared. I never saw my books again, and maybe my parents

threw them in the garbage, which in my family is practically a sin, to throw away a book as though it were a chicken bone. We Jews, after all, kiss our prayer books when we see them again each Sabbath, after the long week apart, and we venerate our holy Torah so much that if we merely drop it on the floor, we fast for forty days, and when it wears out, from so much reading, we hold a funeral for it, like a person.

I also gave my parents pamphlets about the New Jersey chapter of the Parents and Friends of Lesbians and Gays, but the idea of attending a meeting mortified them. "Why would we talk to strangers about our problems?" my mother said. "We'd have nothing in common with those people." The kind who would bring up a gay daughter, who probably weren't even Jewish.

Except they were. Back home in Boston, I got a call from a woman named Meryl Epstein. She'd looked me up. Her father had recently joined my parents' congregation, and since I had a reputation as a gay activist, and my parents were known for their liberal convictions and activism on the town Democratic committee, she wondered if my father would talk to hers, who'd been in a rage since she had introduced him to her girlfriend. My father agreed to help. He met Mr. Epstein for coffee. He said all the right things: "She is your daughter and you should love her for who she is. She's her own person, making her own decisions, and you should be proud."

To me he wrote a letter: "I cannot accept this lifestyle. I wasn't brought up that way."

I fumed as I read. What would Mr. Civil Rights say to someone who told him, "I cannot accept *black people*. I wasn't brought up that way"? What if they said *Jews*? I didn't write back.

Our silent agreement was silence. Each weekend my parents and I spoke on the phone, in minimalist monosyllables. *How are you? Fine.* Every once in a while, for variety, I might say *I have a cold* or *I went to a play.* I hated those calls. They made my life sound so empty and boring.

**The Witch.**　My niece Rachel was born on December 20, 1988, and in an instant, I was an aunt. I had never felt aunt-like; I bore no resemblance to my own aunts, with their bleached, helmet-like hair, their lipstick-tipped cigarettes, and their Bronx accents. (My mother pounced when any hint of Jersey crept into our speech, insisting we pronounce the t's in "mittens" and "twenty.") My sister Priscilla had given birth at the old St. Margaret's Hospital in Dorchester, which was only about ten minutes from my apartment, so at my mother's urging, I visited Priscilla the next day, the first family member to do so from either side. I wasn't as close to her then as I am now, so I felt awkward about showing up so soon, but as exhausted as she was, she welcomed me as though I belonged and put Rachel in my arms. She remembers it too: "You were the first to see her."

"Besides you."

"Well, yes."

"And Chris."

"Chris, of course. But then you."

Holding the beautiful baby, I felt like the witch at the christening, the one who curses the Sleeping Beauty. Not that I intended to curse my niece—God forbid—but perhaps the witch can't help her malign influence either. Forgotten, uninvited, she shows up anyway, unintentionally casting a shadow over everyone's happy time.

I fantasized that Rachel and I would form a special bond, because she was the oldest and so was I, because I held her first. Roberta, my dear life-partner, started calling her my "double," because the child looked so much like me.

Maybe, I thought, she would become a lesbian.

I realized, even as I thought it, that this hope—this fear—was ridiculous, its purpose to assign myself a more central role in Rachel's life than I in fact played. Because the truth is, I was marginal. I babysat occasionally; I showed up for birthdays. But

I was busy, wrapped up in my own life. And then Priscilla and her family moved to Connecticut, no longer within dropping-in distance. I was lucky that Rachel and her little brothers recognized me from one visit to the next.

Even so, her birth changed my life.

This had nothing to do with her or me or our relationship. But my parents' anxieties dissipated, now that they had a grandchild, and gradually I found myself welcomed back into the fold.

So *that* was the problem all along? Grandchildren? How could I have been so dense, not to have understood that?

Of course my parents, particularly my mother, naturally—or, should I say, because of her socially constructed gender expectations—had longed for grandchildren. This conventional desire, combined with their horrified response to the revelation, after the Second World War, of the extent of the Nazi Holocaust, convinced them that they, like all Jews, had a religious obligation to restore the world Jewish population. Somehow I'd always thought they'd meant this as symbolic, not actionable, surrounded though I was by my five younger siblings. For my parents, a lesbian could never be a good Jewish daughter—the fact that my cohort of lesbians was reproducing at a great rate being either unknown to them or perhaps worse than if we'd been having no children at all. And actually, some parents did react as my friend Ellen's had, shunning her after her partner had a baby, causing her years of terrible hurt and depriving themselves of the *naches in di kinder,* the joy of children, to which all Jewish grandparents are entitled. My parents would never have done such a thing, but let's be honest: neither would they have taken such a child to their hearts. They would have been polite.

The thing is, though, I've always known I'd never have children—and this feeling, this sense of my identity, is even more firmly rooted than my sexuality. When I was growing up I did plenty of mothering of my brothers and sisters, although I was never much good at it: I accidentally stuck the babies' soft thighs with diaper pins, and they wouldn't stop crying. The older kids mocked and defied me, and I chased them around the house. I couldn't figure out how to clean up their messes. I fell apart at illnesses and accidents. I got bored. One of my earliest memories is of lying in my bed and hearing my mother get up to deal with a feverish, crying child. That she knew just what to do I found amazing. It terrified me to imagine myself in her place. At the same time I identified with her completely. There were days when, exhausted, depressed, she cried out that we treated her like a mother-machine.

"Oh, no, Mom, we're sorry. We love you. You're not a machine," we would say, desperate to apologize.

"You are inconsiderate, inconsiderate children," she'd insist furiously, about whatever we'd broken or forgotten. Then she would start cleaning up after us or turn to trudge up the stairs.

"Stop, Mom. We'll do it. We'll get it."

"You lost your chance," she'd say. There was no atoning, no going back.

A therapist once asked me, "Didn't that make you angry?"

"No," I realized—and to make that discovery must have been the reason I had gone to see the therapist in the first place, because after that session I didn't go back. "Never. I still feel terrible about it. Poor Mom."

Or maybe I never had kids because it just worked out that way: I was involved in other things; I didn't have the time or the money. Richard occasionally teased me that I would become the mother of his children, but the notion was mostly either a joke or a way to annoy his insane father—an unwed Jewess, a dyke, what would you even call the little bastard? I would maintain at dinner parties that the begetting of children was a great area for gay male–lesbian cooperation. The gay men, to my surprise, were unenthusiastic, especially if their paternity had to remain anonymous. They didn't want to lose track of their offspring or in the worst case be dunned for child support. If they were to inseminate, they wanted to be dads. I thought they were selfish. This was all before AIDS.

But then, I was often surprised by the parents of my generation: that they found their babies hilarious, for one thing. They could sit around watching and laughing at their toddlers for hours. My mother didn't act as though having infants around the house was *fun,* exactly.

And that their desire for children went so deep. I gradually understood that people like my sister Priscilla or my friend Betsy would never feel their lives were fulfilling and complete without kids. This emotion I found utterly foreign—odd, I know, given that women are propagandized about motherhood in so many ways all the time, but somehow I never felt it applied to me. Because I never felt I was a woman. Not in a bad way—just that the quaint notion of the homosexual as the "third sex" resonates.

Meanwhile, there was my dear old friend—former lover, actually—Betsy becoming increasingly desperate as monthly insemination sessions failed to produce results, even when she prepared for them by making a small offering to a fertility goddess she'd picked up in a botanica somewhere. Assuming the receptive, hip-opening *ananda balasana,* or "happy baby" yoga pose, didn't help either. She took several courses of hormones that left her feeling bloated, headachy, and depressed, and will have god-knows-what consequences as she ages, and finally asked me if I would donate an egg. She'd already started discussing sperm with our friend Eric Rofes, whose size, hairiness, and controlling nature gave the impression that he was bursting with masculine fertility and certainly more promising than the unassuming hippie boy she'd found for her original attempts. I was happy to participate, but my blood tests at the fertility doctor's revealed that I was perimenopausal, even though I was only in my late thirties.

Which was ironic, because during my early heterosexual period, I had been so intent on not getting pregnant, using the
pill and a diaphragm and insisting on condoms, all at the same
time, if possible. Before we went to bed, my favorite college
boyfriend had said, "Don't worry. I can help out if you ever need
an abortion." And that may sound awful to some people, but it
is still one of the most reassuring things anyone has ever said
to me. Now it turned out I'd probably never been very fertile.
Hot flashes plague me to this day.

And despite Roberta's never-to-be-slaked curiosity about
what my little offspring would have looked like, all of this was
really for the best, since taking the hormone supplements
required to donate an egg would surely have additionally messed
up my system, and since I had a completely unrealistic notion
of what it would have meant to have a child who was genetically
but not in any other way mine running around in the world. I
had no intention of ever informing my family about what I'd
done; but of course it would hardly have been fair, or possible,
to keep secret from the child the facts of his or her heritage
and additional biological family members, or from my parents
the news of their . . . grandchild? Or something. Even though
it would only have caused them massive confusion.

Suddenly I realize I've never told my mother—or anyone—
about my unfitness, my want of the mothering impulse. It's not
that I've been trying to keep it secret; I've just always thought
it was so obvious it didn't bear mentioning.

Many nieces and nephews followed Rachel. Her brothers,
Zach and Duncan. David's two girls, Maddy and Lucy. Josh's
Teddy and Lindsey, the youngest, were born just over a year
apart, and Josh and his wife Kerry had them both christened at
the same time. Of course my family all attended the ceremony,
although we felt unsure of how to behave in a church and of
what kinds of presents to supply. Up at the altar, Josh looked
joyful, with his new daughter in his arms and his little son

standing beside him, as the priest muttered over them and dabbed their heads with water.

Afterward, in the parking lot, my father took my arm as we walked to his car. "When we heard about you I thought, 'My mother is spinning in her grave,'" he said. "Now, she's spinning the other way!"

Balance, apparently, had been restored: lesbian daughters, Catholic grandchildren. My parents and I still have our differences—sex, the rights of the Palestinian people. But we manage, as families do. We deny, we prevaricate, we talk about the weather. We, too, are turning.

## An Old Joke.

I am a serious person, so when I found myself growing up in a family that went to temple on Friday evenings and sent me to Hebrew school twice a week, I immersed myself in the religion. Even after my bat mitzvah, I continued to take classes with our rabbi, and every Sunday morning, together with the rabbi's daughters, I took the bus into New York and changed to the subway to go to the Jewish Theological Seminary. I loved knowing my way around the city and being probably the only student at Rutherford High School—the only non-rabbi's daughter, anyway—with a pocket full of tokens and the ability to recite all the stops on the uptown Broadway local between 42nd and 116th. I still have the diploma I received from the Hebrew high school program, which is headed "*B'Ezrat HaShem*"—"with the help of the Name"—the holy Name we do not pronounce nor write, apparently even on a document that affirms His participation.

And because of this extensive Jewish education, when I used to attend services I was one of only a handful of congregants who actually understood the prayers we were repeating: me and the rabbi and a few ancients who wandered the aisles and *davened* shrilly at breakneck speed. As soon as I left my parents' home, during my freshman year of college, I began to keep kosher, which released me from both the college cafeteria and my mother's unfortunate cooking. My parents found this reversal of the traditional situation endlessly amusing: "*We'll* have to change the dishes when our *daughter* comes to visit!" I didn't see what was so funny, and eventually my father would concede, "Your grandmother would buy only kosher chickens. She said the nonkosher ones had a bad smell."

"It's true," agreed my mother. "But the kosher butcher is so expensive."

"It's a spiritual practice," I said. "To bless our food. To become aware of it as we eat."

"Of course, it's very healthy," said my mother.

Then in my sophomore year, as I stood next to my parents and brothers and sisters at Yom Kippur services, the congregation admiring our long row of Hoffmans as we beat our breasts and confessed to terrible crimes that we hadn't committed, I thought, as I examined my soul, "What the *fuck* am I doing?" and walked out. At home I made an excellent sandwich—pastrami on marble rye, my mother must have made a special trip to the deli to prepare for breaking the fast—left a note on the kitchen counter, packed my bags, headed for the bus stop.

My apostasy—in Yiddish *apikores,* meaning not just any old heretic but an educated one who should know better—exiled me from the tradition I'd so diligently studied, and indeed from the entire history of the Jews. The rabbis instruct parents to tell the wicked child, on Passover: "We celebrate this seder because of what God did for us, when He rescued our people from Egypt. For us, but not for you. If you had been there, you would have been left behind." Harsh, especially for a kid, but that's how the Old Ones thought. No one gets a pass. If I forget thee O Jerusalem let my tongue cleave to my palate. And I not only forget Jerusalem, I spit on it. What has it ever done for us, but cause bloodshed and grief? The Arabs want it so much, I say let them have it.

After that Yom Kippur, although I might humor my parents by attending services with them when I visited, I wouldn't, couldn't, open my mouth. The words were no longer mine to chant, although I possessed their meaning. There's a verse from the psalms that we repeat silently, before the silent prayer itself: *Lord open my lips, and my mouth will sing your praises.* And I believe that, if nothing else, to be true: with every breath we express our miraculous essence. But my lips were sealed.

My mother's mother had died when I was ten, and when my three remaining grandparents died during my first few years of college, I came home barely long enough to attend their funerals.

It's not that my school was far away—in fact, it was about half an hour by car from the town where I grew up. Except that I didn't have a car; I didn't even drive, because in my high school, the driver's ed teacher was also the football coach, so only the guys on the team ever got a chance to practice in the school car, and my father's attempts to teach me had not, to put it mildly, been a success. He's impatient. And I tend to confuse left and right when someone is yelling at me. Even with no car, though, buses ran frequently enough so the trip wasn't particularly difficult.

And it's not that I was an excessively dedicated student—rather the opposite, owing to the coincidence of having absorbed both my high school's credo of sit-down-and-shut-up and the ethos of the 1960s, which confirmed my experience that school wasn't about learning at all but rather was a conspiracy to police youthful minds. I rejected grades and tests, I cut my lectures, I went instead to screenings of French films and poetry readings and SDS meetings, where I said not a word but dutifully showed up whenever there was a call for a demonstration—against the war, in support of the people. When the workers in a nearby factory walked out, SDS sponsored regular carpools to the picket line, where we chanted, "Boycott Fedders! Support the strike!"

Walking down the street even now, I sometimes find myself humming our slogan. Fedders manufactured air conditioners, so as far as I was concerned, it was like calling for a boycott of mink coats or caviar. I wished the company's product had been something humbler and more daily: something I would have been more likely to buy and could thus have sacrificed.

And it's not even that I loved college so much. Frankly, I couldn't figure out what I was doing there. I had decided that since I read so many books—anything my teachers had not assigned—there was no point in majoring in English; I should do something I wasn't naturally inclined to do on my own, like experimental psychology. American history. Music. Comparative religion. Eventually, my favorite time of the semester became the reading period before winter exams, when I could stop floundering around and simply sit in the library day after day, taking notes on my textbooks and staring out the window at the snow silently filtering onto the evergreens.

About a month into my first semester, my mother's father had a stroke. Impulsively, my mother had visited him only the week before, taking with her my youngest sister and brother, Becky and Josh. It was strange—that she should have had an impulse, and followed it. And then he was gone. Years later I said to my mother, "We're lucky, we don't have a lot of heart disease in our family."

"What do you mean?" she said. "Look at my father."

"He died in his sleep at eighty-four," I said. "We should all have such heart disease, Ma."

In contrast, my father's mother's death was terrible. She had been sick with Alzheimer's disease for years, devastating everyone who knew her because of the deterioration of her brilliant mind and the sapping of her prodigious energy. The nieces on that side of the family are all named in her honor: Rachel Rose, Zoë Rose, Erica Rose. My grandfather survived for only a few months without her, then he died too, of a stroke.

Not a day goes by, my father often says, when he doesn't think of his parents, when he doesn't miss them.

Oddly, I've begun to feel the same.

When they died, I was an adolescent. It was the unchanging nature of grandparents to be old, to speak with strange accents, to die. My relationships with them had been formal and awkward—even with my mother's mother, who had filled in as a supplemental caretaker for us when we were infants. There are family stories about it: how she castigated my mother for not feeding us enough, because we were all so skinny. How she forced bananas, classically baby's first food, on my brother David, who had an allergy to them that caused him to vomit all over her. Yet this primal experience had not created a bond. As I grew older, my grandparents and I hadn't known what to say to each other.

And when they died, my behavior was callous. Perhaps assuming that my parents' relationships with them were as distant as mine, I failed to perceive their sorrow. I didn't comfort them, I just hung around the funerals looking sullen. My dress itched. When the service was over, I couldn't wait to catch the bus back to what I thought of as my life. My real life. My own. The one I was carving out in utter distinction from my existence amid my brothers and sisters and parents and grandparents.

Here's what I mean. On my second day at college, my parents called me on the dormitory phone, and a girl whose name I hadn't learned yet answered it and handed me the receiver. When their familiar voices greeted me, tears sprung to my eyes. With great effort, I suppressed them. When I remember that brief moment I'm filled with regret—couldn't I at least have told them the simple truth: "I miss you"? But there were so many things about myself I didn't yet know—really basic things. I thought I'd left home. I thought I was an adventurer who would travel the world. I didn't know that just about any form of transport except a bicycle or my own two feet made me feel ill. I had no idea that I couldn't read a map if my life depended on it. With my parents to guide me, I hadn't needed to.

After that moment in the phone booth, I rarely allowed myself to visit or even to call. I introduced my parents to my friends only if they were extremely disreputable. Yet my parents were loving and kind and carefully respectful of my independence, which made my struggle even more confusing. Somehow I could not be both with them and with myself.

Coming out solved that problem. I finally hit upon something that made my parents feel as awkward with me as I had come to feel with them—especially when I started working at *Gay Community News,* developed a minor public reputation, got political about it, so it was no longer a matter of we-just-want-you-to-be-happy-sweetheart. But *of course* I got political about it: wasn't that exactly what I'd learned from the examples of my parents and grandparents, who had proudly dedicated their lives to socialism and the establishment of the state of Israel? Justice, justice, you shall pursue! Although our alienation forced me and my parents to recognize ourselves as separate entities, which at least subconsciously was what I'd been going for, it puzzled me. Why were they so disappointed in me, when I'd adopted exactly their values? Maybe I took it all further than they were comfortable with. But who taught me to think that way in the first place? And isn't that the role of the younger generation?

At the beginning of the Passover seder we say, "All who are hungry, let them come and eat," and a designated seder guest opens the front door, to symbolically welcome the hungry people. When my brother David was in high school, he had his goofy friend Doug stand at the door. A hungry person! We scrunched together and made a space for him at the table, even though it was just supposed to be a prank.

Then at the end of the seder, the guests traditionally bless each other by saying, "Next year in Jerusalem"—but we don't mean Jerusalem the city, but rather what the rabbis call Jerusalem Above. The Jerusalem of the spirit, the end of Diaspora. The homecoming of the exile. The opening of the door.

Before Rachel was born it was as though I'd been standing outside the door, waiting for it to open.

So, here I am. *Hineni,* as we learned to respond in Sunday school when our names were called, because thus did our father Abraham identify himself to the Almighty. I'm reclaiming my past. If I find myself in a *shul,* I sing out. I even *daven* a little, for the nostalgia, the beauty of it. I've gone back to reading the right-hand, Hebrew side of the page. It's not like I forgot how.

I'm reclaiming the history of the Jews. I've decided I have as much of a right to it as anyone—even with my bent sexuality, my revolving grandmother, the whole *megillah.* I'm old enough, after all, to have been personally acquainted with the immigrant generation: I was their *shayne maidele,* their *ketzeleh,* their *bubeleh*—their pretty little girl, their kitty, their dolly. My younger brothers and sisters were hardly out of infancy, so what do they know? Only what they've been told, while I actually remember the first time around for all those stories my father has been repeating at every seder since the Kennedy administration. And I wonder, Why those stories? Why not others? I've tried to dig up the facts; I've looked up the records, the ship manifests, but between the immigration officers' contempt and mistakes, and the immigrants' deceptions and confusion, they're more like dreams than information.

Like the old joke. An elderly Jew introduces himself: "Sean Ferguson."

His new friend bursts out laughing. "If you're Sean Ferguson, I'm *Eliyahu ha-Navi*"—Elijah the Prophet come again.

The Jew shrugs. "When we got off the boat, they kept reminding me, 'They'll ask your name. You're not Moysheleh anymore, you're Marvin. Speak English.' I got to the head of the line, and the fellow shouted, 'Name!' and I was so *farmisht,* so mixed up, I said to him, '*Shayn fargessen.*'"

"Sean Ferguson. Next!"

These days, Sean's memory isn't so good. The name by which his dear mother called him, in Yiddish, in English? *Shayn fargessen,* he sighs. I forgot already.

We think history is a science, but mostly it's simply unknowable, even our own, utterly gone, and all that's left are guesswork and imagination. We fill in the best we can.

## at the lake #1

Among the members of Temple Beth-El, remembering the names of the Hoffman kids was practically a party game, like listing all seven dwarfs. There are six of us. Oldest to youngest: Amy, David, Judy, Priscilla, Rebecca, Joshua. Add to that my parents, and our interrelationships are nearly innumerable, eight to the nth degree. In my generation of middle-class Jews, being that prolific just wasn't done, and my parents have never given a plausible explanation for their fecundity. It couldn't have been their original plan, and I know they weren't uninformed about birth control, because my mother has always told the story of having to move to New Haven when my father was in the army and sent to Yale to learn Japanese. She asked her new landlady for the name of a gynecologist, and the landlady said, "This is Connecticut."

Appalled at being mistaken for a completely other kind of person, my mother said, "I'm a married woman!"

"Of course you are, dear," said the landlady. "But this is Connecticut."

The diaphragm was illegal in the state until the Supreme Court's *Griswold v. Connecticut* decision legalizing birth control there, in 1965. Thus is my mother a part of history. She and I have even marched together for reproductive rights, or tried to. At the big March for Women's Lives in Washington in 1992, she took the bus with New Jersey NOW, which shows just how

Serena and Sigmund Hoffman, wedding photograph, September 15, 1945.

deeply she felt about it, since signing up for buses and marching around is not the kind of thing she usually does. I, more typically, drove down from Boston with friends—although I had to get excused from jury duty to do it. I told the judge I had a long-standing commitment to visit my mother, although I didn't tell him where. She and I had picked a corner on which to meet, but it turned out to be impossible to find each other in the crowd. Still, we had the intention, and we were both there at the same time.

On the block where I grew up, in Rutherford, New Jersey, the neighbors were all Catholic, and ours was the smallest family around. The Hetzels had fifteen kids, the Iwanskis had twelve, the Owens next door had seven, and a few houses down they'd started out with a set of triplets, indistinguishable boys with red hair and freckles, all called Trip. So maybe my parents lost their sense of proportion. There was their belief about repopulating the Jewish people. Be fruitful and multiply—it's the first of the 613 commandments in our scripture, the most basic. But wouldn't the principle be drowned out as the house fills up with screaming children and money gets tight? And were they the only ones around to fulfill this *mitzvah,* this righteous deed?

Then there's my mother's claim that she was never happier than when pregnant, and that she loved having an infant to feed and cuddle. The problems begin, she says, when the child starts to talk. But you can't keep replacing the aged-out baby with a new one every two years. Can you? She's proud of having breast-fed all of us, even in the fifties when it was generally thought to be primitive and icky—and then I sucked my thumb until I was ten years old, which the breast-feeding was said to preclude, and we didn't seem to acquire many immunities, either, since we regularly came down with everything that was going around—not just the usual earaches, colds, and 24-hour viruses but also chicken pox, measles, tonsillitis, flu, and German measles, fortunately on a non-pregnant off-year.

We had allergies too: eczema, hay fever. Priscilla's reaction to fish can put her in the hospital. I'd pick up the illnesses first at school and spread them to the little kids, who never seemed to get as sick as I did, so as I lay miserable and undemanding, they needed to be constantly amused during their quarantines.

With so many children in the neighborhood, we played many mass games: hide-and-seek in the late-spring dusk, the fireflies blinking among us as we ran, the kid who was It calling us together at the end of each round, "All-ee, all-ee, in-free"; sledding in the winter, right down the middle of the street, with a lookout at the bottom of the hill chanting the warning, "Car, car, C-A-R, stick your head in a jelly jar"; Wiffle ball in the fall; war, any time. An assortment of Owens, Hetzels, Iwanskis, etc., would gather at either end of the sidewalk in front of our house, chalk a line on the slates, dare us: "Stay off my *propity*!" Or sometimes, "You're going to *purgatory*!" I didn't know what either word meant, but I got the general idea. Capitalism and religion.

When I was seven (and David five, Judy three, and Priscilla eight months) my family took three weeks of summer vacation. For the first week, we went with my father's parents, and my Aunt Norma, Uncle Bud, and their kids to a beach on Lake Erie, which at the time was unpolluted, warm, and shallow. My cousin Elissa, six years older, would take my hand and walk me way, way out, and the water would still be lapping at our knees when we turned to wave to my mother, sitting on a blanket with the baby, dots on the sand. Ronnie, Elissa's older brother, into jazz, led us nightly in a cheer:

"Who's the best?"

"Da-a-ve Brubeck!"

"Who's the worst?"

"Da-a-ve Hoffman!"

"All right, now, stop that," said my mother.

For the second week of our vacation, we went to the Jersey

Shore, where the mosquitoes were so vicious that my mother wouldn't let us leave the cabin, even for a minute, until she'd slathered us from head to toe with a repellent bug-repellent called 6-12. So I didn't much like the shore, until our last day there, when some townie kids showed me how to jump into the breaking waves and, arms stretched in front of me and legs stretched back, ride them until I beached myself on the sand. It was like flying, like Superman on TV—who they say flew lying on his belly on a table, which was then erased from the picture. Once I learned to ride the waves, I never wanted to leave.

We still had a final week of vacation left, though, at Lake Buel, in Great Barrington, Massachusetts—a retreat recommended to my parents by their friends the Epsteins, from our temple. We rented a little brown cottage at the end of a rocky dirt road from the elderly Captain and Mrs. Roth, the Captain so-called not because he'd ever had anything to do with the navy—he was in the garment business—but because of the hat he wore puttering around his waterfront, white with a blue life-ring insignia. A few times I saw the old man's penis peeking out from his bathing trunks and didn't know where to look. The Roths had a dock on the lake, from which we swam and caught bluegills, or launched their wooden rowboat and paddled in hilarious circles. My parents thought it was paradise, and the next summer the Roths sold them the place.

And that was it. Every summer after that, as soon as school let out, we drove to the lake. My mother and we kids stayed until Labor Day, and my father, like all dads, came up on weekends, just as though we were at a bungalow in the Catskills.

Our cottage was actually a converted garage. Downstairs it had a little screened-in porch with a picnic table and benches that took up its entire area. You walked inside to the living room, which had come to us furnished, including a roll-top desk with millions of cubbies and a tongue-in-groove cover that we were *not* to play with by sliding it open and shut over and over. A real antique, we thought; it must be worth a fortune, it was so old and cunningly made. On the desk was a lamp with an octagonal, stained-glass shade, each panel of which showed the same brass scene of a lighthouse and a sailboat, backed by a different cracked sunset. I loved to contemplate it: it was impossible to decide which scene I liked best—the rose, the green, the magenta and orange swirl? But it didn't matter, they were all there. But which was best? Several winters ago the lamp disappeared, perhaps stolen by some kids who broke in, or perhaps, rumors flew among the siblings, it was one of us. To replace it, my mother bought a Plexiglas fake-Tiffany at KMart.

Up a steep set of stairs was an attic with exposed rafters, a light bulb dangling from the ceiling, one small window in the front—the kids' room. Later, a second upstairs bedroom for David and Josh was somehow tacked onto the back of the house, and the original attic became the girls' room. (Still later, after Priscilla was the first of us to marry, her husband and brother-in-law built yet another addition, in which my parents installed a double bed. My mother infuriated everyone by announcing that it was "the *married*-children's room"; Priscilla renamed it "the boom-boom room.")

The ceiling in the girls' room was so deeply raked that even a child could stand only in the very center of it, in the narrow corridor between the beds, two on each side. Mine was adjacent to the window, and on certain August mornings, the wind rattling the torn shade was so heady with the fragrance of the white pines surrounding the house that I would lean out of my bed and halfway out the window, to breathe it in, until one of my sisters would ask what I was doing, and I would pull my head back inside. The cottage floors, walls, and ceilings were all made of the same pine boards, whose knots composed themselves into faces evil and kind, human and animal, as I stared—especially at bedtime, when my mother read us a chapter from

*Winnie the Pooh* or *Charlotte's Web,* sang "Over the Rainbow," and then pulled the string to turn off the light.

When my father's parents started coming to us for the summer, my parents gave them the downstairs bedroom and moved to the pull-out couch in the living room. In fact, the cottage was infinitely expandable: one summer, in addition to my family and grandparents, my twin cousins Betty and Bobby, who had become hippies, piled in for several days with some of their friends and lovers, unrolling their sleeping bags on the kitchen floor. And for several years in a row, our rabbi and his wife and three daughters showed up to camp in the front yard. They were kosher, so they kept their food in big coolers and did their own cooking on a grill; but the problem was the bathroom, for which there was always a line. "Forget becoming a doctor," my mother advised us in contravention of the stereotypical advice. "Be a plumber."

Each morning my grandparents sipped mugs of hot water, sometimes with a translucent slice of lemon floating on top, an Old World digestive invented by a people who couldn't afford a few flakes of tea, a crumb of sugar. Of course, here tea was plentiful. They drank it after their hot water. My grandfather would spoon sugar into his—three, four spoonfuls.

"Why don't you stir it, Pa?" asked my father.

"Nah, nah. Too svit."

My grandmother sweetened hers with cherry jam, giving my father, when he worked in the lab at General Foods in Hoboken, the idea for a line of flavored teas: cherry, strawberry, marmalade, grape. "No one else went along with it. But now look," he says. "in the supermarket, everywhere. There's Snapple."

During the summer before my bat mitzvah, my grandfather, who used to make a little extra cash during the Depression by preparing boys to lead the service, helped me to study. We sat next to each other at the table on the porch, and my mother remembers the two of us together so happily and sentimentally that it makes my adolescent boredom seem worthwhile. In fact, the arrangement made both my grandfather and me uncomfortable. He was quiet, impatient, perfectionist, and I didn't please him, stumbling every day over the same words. As he corrected me I memorized his lips, the color of old pencil erasers, and his big nostrils. His mouth made a wet, ticking sound before he spoke that would send a shiver down my spine. I had seen his false teeth and my grandmother's, each in its own glass of water, on their night table.

Perhaps he too would have preferred to be doing something else—scraping down the house and repainting it brown, walking his two daily miles down the road and back, unhooking bluegills from David's fishing line and carrying them in a plastic bucket to the side of the house, cleaning and grilling them for breakfast.

During my adolescence, family summers at the lake began to bug me more and more. If we had to have a New England getaway, I grumbled to myself, then we should retreat deeper into the woods, observe nature, strip away material things, like Thoreau, whose stuttered "Simplify! Simplify! Simplify!" was my favorite passage in *Walden*. Failing that, I thought, we should just stay home in New Jersey, where I at least had a few friends. At the lake, I spent every morning writing to them. The most important part of my day was the walk down the dirt road to the mailbox, which at the time had a red tin flag the postman raised to show there were letters inside. Once we all outgrew adolescence, the box rusted through and fell off its post.

Of course, no one on our road could have survived in the woods. We were all Jewish, inept. The Captain and Mrs. Roth arrived first and established an outpost; then, as the *goyim* fled throughout the late fifties, they were joined by others of our ilk from the Jersey suburbs. So Lake Buel was not a tinkering, bird-watching kind of place. My study-house ancestors—what would they have known of building a dock, scraping the moss off the roof, sealing the floors against mice, the attic against raccoons? We roared around the lake in motorboats, which we had no idea how to service. We enjoyed the animals and plants, the rustling in the underbrush, the flashes of color, the chirping, the pretty leaves and flowers and berries, but we couldn't tell one from another. Adam gave names to every living thing in the Garden, but the Jews have forgotten them all.

My grandfather, at least when it came to putting together and repairing, was an exception. He came to this country never having been to a secular school, just some backward yeshiva— but in one year he completed his American high school diploma, math his best subject, and after stints at the Ford Motor Company and elsewhere, got a job as a draftsman, making technical drawings for the Buffalo Forge Company. He bought a two-family house on East Ferry Street in Buffalo, which he maintained beautifully. During one of my father's school vacations, my grandfather insisted that my father help him to pour a concrete floor in the basement. With my father observing, my grandfather measured out the area with sticks and string, mixed the concrete, checked its lay with a carpenter's level. The floor was perfect.

"How did he know how to do all that?" I ask my father.

"Who knows?" he says. "He knew."

My father counts: he's owned five houses in his life, and except for the one in Great Barrington, which both he and my mother feel is perfect in every way and thus never in need of updating or repair, they all made him anxious. The shingles fell from the roofs, the basements flooded, the lawns became infested with crabgrass and dandelions. "At least they're green," my mother said. Now the two of them live in a cramped apartment, and my father feels a burden has been lifted. It turns out that my sister Becky inherited all the common sense in the family. She hangs pictures, she installs computers, she programs the VCR, and years ago when our sister Judy married He-Who-Shall-Not-Be-Named, from whom she's now divorced, Becky built them a round dining-room table for a wedding present and then arranged to have it shipped to them in Chicago, where they had settled.

My mother loves having a daily *routine*—possibly her favorite word—and at the lake, this is how it went: mornings were for cleaning the house and errands in town. We kids were to play outside; when I was young, I spent the time wandering in the woods, occasionally coming across lewdly shaped mushrooms in lurid colors poking out from the mulch, which creeped me out, so I would cut my hike short and quickly retrace my steps home. My father had an army buddy, Phil Satrapi, who lived up in Pittsfield. He'd occasionally drive over with his wife, bringing jars of mushrooms he and his wife had foraged and put up, causing much hilarity among the adults about potential misidentifications. "Delicious," said my mother. "At least we'll die happy." I hated Phil Satrapi and his questionable mushrooms, his dingy fishing hat, his off-color jokes; sometimes when I walked through the woods I chanted, "*philsatrapiphilsatrapiphil*" until his name became nonsense, to ward him off.

After lunch, everyone was to go down to the dock. My parents had bought, along with the cottage, a strip of waterfront. They'd had a steep path bulldozed to it, a move they immediately regretted, since the bulldozer indiscriminately tore out the trees and mountain laurel bushes, leaving an ugly scar on the hillside—although over the years, the vegetation has kindly regrown. Every afternoon, my mother clambered down this path with us, even during her pregnant summers, horrifying the neighbors and my grandmother, who rarely ventured down it herself. She stayed in the cottage, wrapped in sweaters, insisting it was too cold to go out. Surrounded by trees, the cottage was dark and damp, even on the sunniest days, but persuading my stubborn grandmother that she'd feel better outside was often—although not always—impossible. On the rare afternoons that she joined us, she would put on a voluminous bathing suit and wade into the water up to her knees, lean over, and pat a few drops on her chest and arms.

"See, Mom," my mother would call to her mother-in-law, "It's not so bad."

"*Ach, a mechiah!*" my grandmother would agree. A miracle of refreshment. The Native Americans had called the area Mahaiwe—what else could this word be, said the adults, but Indian for *mechiah*?

"You're so lucky," my parents admonished us. "We could never afford to send all of you to camp." But had we asked to go to camp?

I read, and the words in my head silenced the voices around me. I babysat up and down the road, to give myself something to do and a few dollars for when we finally returned home. My brothers and sisters had friends at the lake, but the only kids my age were the Roths' granddaughters from Long Island, whose main amusement was teasing me about my flat chest and the black hairs sprouting under my arms.

The adults tried to shake me from my moodiness. "Always with her nose in a book. Take a little swim, sweetheart."

Great Bore-ington, I thought. There was no escape and no privacy. Even in the bathroom someone was always knocking on the door, and if you decided to leave the dock early and go up to the house, there was Grandma in the living room. Not to mention that somebody always noticed and said, "What, you're going *now*? You'll miss the *best part* of the afternoon!" I paddled a leaky canoe into the middle of the lake, hunkered down across the staves, cracked open *Moby-Dick*—what better book to read on the water, as the canoe rotated slowly in the current or rocked wildly in the wash of a passing motor boat, the most popular type of which was called—what else?—the Boston Whaler.

## my grandmother was sent forth

My mother's mother was sent forth, as God commanded: pick yourself up and go, from your land and from your birthplace. There, they had nothing to give her for the journey but feathers, gathered carefully day by day from the barnyard and the kitchen. Offal, but it was the best they could do. They presented them to her when she left, and with them she was to make a *pereneh,* a featherbed. In the golden country, she'd have a place to lay her head. They hoped she would be able to make her way. She was fourteen, my mother says. Sometimes she says thirteen.

The ship manifest says sixteen, but of course she had lied. No one cared, as long as she gave them something to write on the form: *Saloon, Cabin and Steerage Aliens Must Be Completely Manifested. This Sheet Is for Steerage Passengers. Manifest of Alien Passengers for the U.S. Immigration Officer at Port of Arrival.*

On the boat, she received food. A relative on my father's side once described it for her daughter, who had a tape recorder: "For breakfast we had herring, bread, and tea," she said loudly into the machine. "For lunch, potatoes, cabbage soup, and corn bread." Not fluffy American corn bread, but the Jewish kind, which is like a rye bread, or a rock. "That was considered as a very good meal, since we came from a small town," she concluded. And what could have been smaller than the place my grandmother referred to as Mostyelke—little Mosty, an obscure outskirts, as opposed to Grossmosty, big Mosty, a few miles away. I find a photograph on the Internet that shows Gross-mosty's main square: a dusty corral with some low, ramshackle buildings in the background. Not a human being in sight.

*SS Kaiserin August Victoria. Sailing from Hamburg, 1 May 1907. Arriving Port of New York, 11 May 1907.* The manifest lists a crowd of others like her—children, on their own—and I imagine that they banded together, and so sustained each other during the terrible crossing, the puke and filth. As soon as the ship docked, they scattered into the city, my grandmother's shipboard companions becoming a few more of the many she had once known but would never see again. At the dreadful moment of arrival, she could not have been more alone. She stood on the crowded pier, weighed down by her sack of feathers.

Somewhere on the awful concrete shore were her adult cousins. When she found them, they gave her a place to sleep on the kitchen floor and put her to work. She watched their five little girls, she sewed in a factory, she went to night school to learn English. She sent her earnings home and urged her mother to come to her, but her mother refused. "A Jew can't live there a kosher life," she said. Of course, as it turned out, in Mostyelke a Jew could live no life at all. After the Second World War my grandparents contacted the Red Cross to search for the family members they'd left behind—but they, and their neighbors, and indeed all of Mostyelke *shtetl*, had vanished with barely a trace. My mother shows me a photograph of her grandmother, a small woman wearing a big white apron and a headscarf like a Muslim. "See how your great-grandmother's apron shines," my mother says. It's because of the age of the photograph, but my mother likes to think it's because her grandmother was a marvel among housewives, her laundry famous throughout Jewish Poland. Looking more closely at the photograph, I expect my great-grandmother's face to be old and wizened, but underneath all the scarves and layers is a young wife; when she sent her

"A cousin from Poland," says my mother of this photo. After World War II, her parents tried to find their relatives in Europe, but with no success. This doll-like child was gone and unidentifiable.

daughter across the sea, her skin was unlined, her eyes clear and observant.

In America, my grandmother gave her feathers to a tailor to make the *pereneh,* but his needles kept breaking. "What is wrong with these cursed greenhorn feathers?" he swore. The family had scattered their *groschen,* their pennies, in them for luck, and they bought just about as much luck as they were worth.

She brought the *pereneh* into her marriage. My grandfather, judging by his photographs, was a wavy-haired dandy; in one, he wears a beautiful suit with a pocket square and a watch chain, surrounded by five of his sisters. When his conscription papers had arrived, they'd helped him escape to America. First he did piecework, sewing ties. Then he peddled the ties door to door. The youngest son, he wasn't obliged to send his money home, so he saved, week in and week out, until he had enough to buy a building in the Bronx, on Manor Avenue. The scheme was that the rents would pay the mortgage, except they never did. By the time he bought, it was the Depression. The tenants paid what they could, and he had to be satisfied with that. Apartments all over the city were going begging. He copied other landlords and offered the first month free as an inducement, but then the tenants defaulted altogether when the month was up, sneaking away in the middle of the night.

At his insistence, the couple spoke English in the home. Everything was silence and crossed purposes; they could barely recognize themselves. My grandfather Leybish became Louie, and my grandmother Sheindel, Jennie. Louie and Jennie had three daughters: Toyveh (Toby), Perel (Pearl), and then, ten years later, my mother, a child of their old age. They had prepared no name for the newborn, so her birth certificate reads, "Baby Ginsburg." Then she was to be Sarah, but her sisters objected to such a greenie name; they persuaded their mother to import a syllable from some beautiful place far from their apartment and

My mother's grandmother, Gittel Henna Margolies.

the Bronx, where every other Jewish girl you met was a Sarah. Baby became Serena Ginsburg—to my mother, the name has always sounded absurd.

"What do you mean?" we children would ask her adoringly. "It's *beautiful*." We thought everything about her beautiful: her voice as she chanted the blessing over the candles on Friday evenings, three times circling her hands over the flames, to welcome the Sabbath Queen into our home; her round green eyes; her nose, which had been broken somehow (*how?*) when she was a child and never set. Even today, my father dials the phone and hands her the receiver and says, "Here is your beautiful mother." But she has always believed she is hideous.

"'Ginsburg' doesn't go with 'Serena,'" she tried to explain to us. "'Ginsburg' is a name in a Jewish joke." Ginsburg and Cohen go to the store. We'd never heard such a joke, we thought she must be referring to yet another bygone artifact from her childhood, like the way she'd played potsie instead of hopscotch and never learned to ride a bike. The Christian kids in the playground sometimes yelled at me, "Jesus saves. Moses invests," but it went over my head, and maybe they didn't get it either, they'd heard it from their parents and their parents' friends, standing in the living room, swilling the ice around in their drinks. Har har har.

Even with three daughters, my grandfather didn't believe in educating girls. My grandmother, that may have been a different story. She would have encouraged her daughters in private—but who had privacy? The family lived in a one-bedroom apartment. The three daughters shared two beds, pushed together, and my mother slept in the gap. Her sisters snored and kicked. The beds shifted.

(*I wonder: Did the girls bump up against each other in their crowded bed? Did their legs rub against each other? Did they sleep spoonwise for warmth and the comfort of another's touch? Did my*

*mother alternate which side of the gap she slept on, Toby's one day,*
*Pearl's the next? Did Pearl and Toby massage each other's backs*
*when they came home after a long day at work? What did they talk*
*about as they brushed out their hair? Probably not the way they*
*rolled toward and away from each other in the dark.)*

One night my mother sat up and declared, "The answer to
the problem is—" and fell back to sleep as her sisters hovered
over her and waited for the rest.

"What problem is she talking about?"

"So tell already, the answer?"

But her dream veered off in another direction, and she said
nothing more, and in the morning, she remembered none of
it. Her sisters pummeled her with pillows.

My mother has always dreamed anxiously of failing tests.
It's not unusual for her to discover the answers to problems
in the middle of the night. She is a secret insomniac, which I
understood only when I became an insomniac myself. The clue
is that at breakfast, she would often tell us kids, "In the middle
of the night I realized. . . ." Where I left the keys. How to reor-
ganize the linen closet. What the name was of Judy's kindergarten teacher. As a child, when I complained of not sleeping,
she would tell me, "You only *think* you weren't sleeping. You
were probably dreaming."

Now when I visit, I hear her rustling around the apartment
at 4:00 a.m. She is having a bad night, and I must be too, since
I'm awake to hear her. Although maybe I'm just dreaming that
I'm awake, and that she is awake and moving around outside
my door. Maybe we're both dreaming the same dream.

Finally Toby married and left her side of the mattress.

Whenever my mother and her sisters emerged from their
bedroom they were to be fully clothed, including shoes and
stockings. Barefoot is for mourners. Nobody around here is
dead yet. Their father became apoplectic if they so much as

My mother's father Louis (Leybish) Ginsburg with four of his sisters.

tiptoed to the bathroom in a slip. He did not want to be constantly reminded that all his children were worthless girls, doing girlish things. He never hugged them.

*(Am I reading too much into my grandfather's strictures on modesty if I wonder whether he feared the temptations of a houseful of women, and that was why he made sure never to gaze upon his daughters' bodies or to touch their flesh? Was he protecting them?)*

On Rosh Hashanah and Yom Kippur the girls and their mother dressed up, rummaging at the last minute through their dresser drawers for a kerchief or a piece of lace to pin to their hair. In the synagogue they found seats in the women's balcony, where only those in the very front could glimpse the men praying downstairs and hear the occasional outburst from the cantor. For everyone else, it was bickering all day long, and stomping back and forth:

*"Phew! Effen di vindeh!"* Open the window! *Slam.*

*"Brr! Fermach di vindeh!"* Close the window! *Slam.*

When she met my father's parents, my mother says, they spoke such an unadulterated, educated Yiddish that she was at first embarrassed to say a word to them, and only from them did she learn the proper word for "window": *"fenster."*

My mother went to Cornell University, a story I've heard many times, her great rebellion: how she excelled in all her classes at James Monroe High School, because she figured that if she was so ugly, she'd better become smart; how she refused to go to Hunter College like everyone else and won a full scholarship; how her parents dug up some Ginsburg relative in Ithaca with whom she was to live, since it was humiliating and simply wrong for an unmarried daughter to leave the family; and how Ginsburg unexpectedly picked up and left, freeing her to move into a dormitory where, as in the Bronx, she had two roommates, but a twin bed all her own.

She likes to tell this story on herself: on her first day in the strange rural surroundings, she looked out the window and saw

My mother, Serena Ginsburg, ca. 1929. The family, my mother says, took a vacation to a farm.

a small brown animal hopping across the lawn. "A kangaroo!" she gasped, astonished. Her roommates, upstate farm girls, had hysterics. They'd already torn into her luggage to discover a kosher salami hidden in it by my grandmother just in case and my mother's collection of hats, which she'd trimmed herself.

But, Ma? The Bronx Zoo was founded in 1899, in plenty of time for field trips from the New York City public schools in the 1930s. And haven't you told me you remember farms up in Riverdale? And doesn't a city girl inherently have more fashion sense than two hicks?

They shared the salami and became lifelong friends.

My mother claims that the only bunnies she'd ever seen were in picture books, and those were white with pink ears.

Maybe the farms remained in the distance and the zoo unvisited because of my grandfather's anxieties. He'd gotten so he hated to leave his building, having become convinced that in his absence the boiler would explode. The floors trembled as it rumbled on and off, according to its whim, and every couple of weeks his no-good cousin Ben Ginsburg, a numbers runner and general local thug, would show up and insist on being let down into the basement to add his own fuel to the fire: a sheaf of betting slips.

As a child, my mother would sit on the stoop, playing with her dog Beauty and listening to the neighbors complain all day long about the *landlord*. He was a plague, slow with repairs, no mercy in his heart when the rent came due. In a nutshell, a mean, stingy SOB. Did my grandfather care what they said? He had his mortgage to pay, his own problems. His three daughters. His boiler. The numbers. His little girl showed him a drawing in her picture book of a slavering beast, nothing like her Beauty. I imagine it looked like the rabid creature Atticus Finch shoots dead on the street in *To Kill a Mockingbird*.

"Papa? Dis a *landlord*?"

My mother and her family, in the Hoffman family living room in Rutherford, N.J., early 1960s. Back row, left to right: Pearl, Toby, Serena. Front row, left to right: Jennie Ginsburg, Louis Ginsburg.

He told me the landlord story himself. He would try to amuse us children by scrunching up his face and crying like a baby, but his high sobs embarrassed me. I liked it better when he distributed chocolate-covered donuts. I was about five when I looked up from playing on the street corner, and there he was, carrying a white paper bakery bag.

Some days I'd scuff around in the grass for hours, wishing I could *find* something: a red rhinestone that had fallen off the neighbor's cowgirl costume, a dime, a squashed rubber ball, anything. And then some days, amazing things just happened: my grandfather, with donuts, walking from the bus stop. My grandmother had been staying with us. She had left him—not that I knew that—driven away by his paranoia. He had begun shouting at her and accusing her of deceiving him with other men, of all kinds of crazy things. Perhaps he hit her, too, but of course no one says that. On the day I found him walking from the bus stop, she had phoned him to say she would return. "If he was sick I wouldn't leave him," she told my mother, and my mother told me admiringly, many years later. "So, he is mentally sick." My mother thinks her mother was heroic in her adherence to her marriage vows. She also thinks her mother was foolish and self-destructive. She had gladly taken her in.

Actually my mother's whole family, both sides, was nuts. Faygeh-Rivka, my grandmother's sister, who was diagnosable, had moved into Manor Avenue. I ask my mother, "Where did she sleep? What was it like, living with a schizophrenic? Did she frighten you?"

She shrugs. "My father made a room for her in the basement."

She named my sister Priscilla for her—now why name a child after your delusional aunt? It's what we do. But how do you derive Priscilla from Faygeh? The child was born on Thanksgiving, and Priscilla is an American Thanksgiving name. P, F— in Yiddish it's the same letter, the pronunciation just depends on whether you put in a dot. It's still no name for a Jewish girl. Well, of course not, if you just say "Priscilla." But try rolling the "r" around in the back of your throat, and drawing out the second syllable, and encouraging yourself with a gesture: "*Pr-ris-cee-la.*" See? Jewish!

The first born, I received, as a middle name, the name of my mother's good aunt, Tante Bessie: Beth/Basheh. In the photos she is stout and big-nosed, truly *mies,* poor thing, but her eyes behind the glasses are kind. "*A mieseh ober a guteh,*" my father's mother would have said: homely but kind. On Passover I bake Tante Bessie's apple cake. The recipe as transmitted to me by my mother says first to line the cake pan with a paper bag. You put in matzo meal and eggs, but no milk or butter, since it's *parve,* to serve after the brisket, for dessert. If only the meal were *milchig,* you could rub the pan with the butter's waxed-paper wrapping. The apple cake has no spices, not even a dusting of cinnamon, and it's heavy like a brick, with a texture like the mortar our ancestors the slaves moistened with their tears when they built the pyramids and a taste from the Pale of Settlement. My mother and I are the only ones who eat it. We think it's delicious.

My mother's *meshugeneh* Aunt Faygeh, poor crazy thing, ended her life in the snake pit of King's County Hospital, penniless, her small savings having been pocketed bit by bit by her guardian, her brother Irving, always called *gonef.* Thief, he visited her faithfully, says my mother—and then charged her account for every minute he spent by her side and every cab he took attending to her business. Irving's beautifully shod foot never touched a subway platform, his *tuchis* never settled onto a bus seat. When Faygeh died, he snatched her diamond engagement ring, the only relic of her two-week marriage—"the poor guy probably tried to interfere with her," says my mother—and refused to give it up to Pearl, its intended heir.

Faygeh, like my grandparents and aunts, is buried so far out on Long Island that even my father, who has the sense of direction of a homing pigeon, could never find the cemetery again after their funerals—which has everything to do with the fact that Irving-the-*Gonef* was treasurer of the Grossmosty *landsmenschaft* and burial society to which they all belonged, and surely arranged a deal. Even Irving's own wife and daughters despised and resented him. The family never went anywhere together. He'd arrive at the apartment on Manor Avenue, my mother says, and then an hour or so later the women would come. And then he'd leave, and they'd stay.

I'm ten, clustered with my brother and sisters in a parking lot behind a brick building that looks nothing like a modern hospital and doesn't allow visitors under the age of eighteen. My father points to a window, and we wave like crazy at my mother and the new baby. Or are we waving at my grandmother? Becky was born on the fourteenth of August, and my grandmother died shortly afterward, on the second day of Rosh Hashanah.

My mother stood in the doorway of my bedroom, tears welling in her eyes. "Your grandmother," she said. I'd never before seen my mother cry, and I didn't know what to do. I had no experience of an adult in need of consolation. I sat in my chair with my book on my lap; my mother stood in the doorway. She knelt to hug me. I felt I should cry, too, but I hadn't known my grandmother very well. There were such barriers between us, of language, of experience. I was growing up a safe, beloved, monolingual suburban girl: no pogroms, no poverty, no dirt, no exile, no piecework, no Yiddish, no feathers. We children were admonished to respect our elders. Familiarity was not appropriate.

Still, we had looked forward to visiting my grandparents' apartment. They would take us to a nearby playground, and afterward we were allowed to take turns rocking in their rocking chair and refilling their glasses with seltzer from a blue glass squirt bottle. Gently, gently—no wild rocking to make the chair walk across the floor, and no aiming the seltzer bottle at your brother like on the *Three Stooges*.

No kids allowed at the funeral, either. For days, people we knew from temple crowded into the living room, and the rabbi, with his high polished forehead, led a service while my mother sat on a small cardboard box printed to look like wood. She had covered the mirrors with sheets, and she wore a black button on her collar.

She believes her mother was a victim of malpractice, but in those days what could you do? The doctor was the doctor. He looked in my grandmother's throat and said she had infected tonsils, but as an adult, she should not attempt to have them removed. The next thing anyone knew, she had a gall bladder attack, then the diagnosis was pancreatitis, then she was dead. But a woman shouldn't live long anyway, she used to say, according to my mother. Once she gets too old, she's no good to anyone. You should take her out and shoot her like a horse. Like the decrepit horses of Mostyelke.

I inherited my grandmother's pink flannel nightgown and wore it to shreds. But maybe I misunderstood. Maybe the nightgown arrived in my drawer from another source, only coincident with my grandmother's death. It does seem bizarre to give a child a dead woman's lingerie. Although I received hand-me-down bras when the time came, pointy ones, which I didn't come close to filling, and I should probably be forever grateful that when I started menstruating, my mother didn't give me the traditional slap across the face and produce a worn sanitary belt with strands of elastic worming out of it. Several pairs of my brother's underpants were labeled "Fred Woocher," a boy we didn't even know, and David used to fantasize about meeting him: "Freddy! I never followed in your footsteps, but I walked in your jockey shorts!" He's such a clown.

The bras were good brands, like the other clothes that had belonged to my cousins and my mother's friend's daughters. She would turn out a neckline to show me the label. "Look, Saks! I could never buy you a blouse like this." The sleeves would be short, the cuffs tight. Alternatively, some of the dresses would have accommodated two of my skinny selves.

# the sylvia plath of the lower east side

*an immigrant tragedy*

On his way home from the factory, my grandmother's brother Meyer decides to go for a shave—this is in around 1935, let's say late on a Friday afternoon. Sabbath is approaching, he's just gotten paid, his wife is at home in the apartment, humming while a chicken roasts in the oven and his two little daughters play together, quietly for a change, in a corner of the room. The barber's chair is soft, his towels hot, his razor sharp, and his conversation—baseball, politics—undemanding. Meyer feels a nick, but he waves away the man's apology, tosses him an extra penny, leaves the shop rubbing his smooth cheek appreciatively. Sighing, he imagines being groomed like this every day, instead of scraping at his face over a basin of freezing water in the dark kitchen, while his wife rushes from one end of the room to the other, why, he doesn't know, and his daughters pummel each other.

The next day the little nick starts to throb, and by nightfall he is sweating and thrashing with fever. By morning he is raving—the infection has spread to his brain. Penicillin treatment doesn't exist yet. The funeral is a few days later.

In my mother's photograph album, there is only one picture of this brother of my grandmother's and none of his wife or younger daughter, whose names are forgotten, but there are lots of pictures of Little Pearl, the older girl, apparently a favorite among her cousins. My mother points her out again and again: a child in a white dress happily playing on a tire-swing, sitting on a beach. "Now that's a sad story," my mother sighs. Here's the rest of it:

When Meyer's young wife comes home from the funeral she is distraught. She stands in the kitchen in her black dress. How will they live, with no income and the rent coming due every month and the grocer's bills? She's been worrying the question ever since her husband stopped making sense, and she hasn't found an answer yet, because there is none. She kneels and gathers Little Pearl and her sister into her arms. They whine and squirm and she shakes them hard and cries, "Shah!" in a high, clear voice nothing like her usual resigned mumble. Surprised into stillness, the girls let her hug them more tightly to her. She shifts them into one arm and stretches the other behind her to the oven, pulls down the door, flips on the gas.

# the madorskys come to america

The Moiseyev Dance Company toured the United States for the first time in 1958, to usher in a new era of cultural exchange. My mother, who loves ballet, excitedly gathered the family to watch the special performance on the *Ed Sullivan Show*.

"Come see, Ma," my father called my grandmother. She too enjoyed dancing, as well as singing, acting, performing—doing them, watching them. Her father, she would reminisce, would take her, Rose, his oldest and smartest, in the wagon with him when he traveled from Rogachov to Mogilev. Business finished, they attended the famous Mogilev theater. (Famous in Rogachov, I thought when I heard this story, but the theater is still there and still a tourist destination, with a picture on the Internet—a daunting orange building with a strange bulging tower and about a million wings.) On the way home, they sang over and over the songs they had heard, committing them to memory, and they stayed with my grandmother for the rest of her life, even through the Alzheimer's. Her daughter, my Aunt Norma, would walk with her up and down the hospital corridors, as they sang the old songs together.

Norma tells me this, and I think of my friends Michael Bronski and Walta Borawski, when Walta was in the demented final stages of AIDS, and Michael said, "He barely knows his name, but he could be a contestant on *Opera Quiz*." Music is the last thing to go. Music, and Yiddish: another friend tells me the story of her grandmother, a woman who spoke English for her entire adult life, but who after a stroke could speak only *mamaloschen,* the Mother Tongue.

My grandmother took one look at the TV and stomped out of the room: "*Feh, Cossacks. Pogromchiks.*"

She hated them like poison—although that didn't at all diminish her pride in her knowledge of Russian or her mockery of my grandfather for his poor accent. "Always with their songs about the white birches," she said dismissively, when as a child I pointed at a single, bright tree. Sterile, spindly things. In her yard was a peach tree. That was a tree. It flowered in the spring and produced sour, wormy fruits in the fall. With a small, sharp knife she cut away the holes and bruises, steamed off the skins, made preserves.

But pogroms were not what had driven her family out, or at least they were not the immediate cause. "The pogroms in Russia of 1881 to 1883 did not spread to Belarus," explains a history text. Of course, attacks of all kinds on Jews were constant before, during, and after that period; it's just that the government, for whatever reason, didn't allow them to rise to the level of riots at that time. Instead, the family's problem was economic. My grandmother's father, Isaac, a big wheeler-dealer, had the idea to borrow a lot of money and build a five-story office building, named for himself: The Madorsky. Brick, maybe it's still standing, like the theater. But he'd overreached. The lender demanded his vig—*the Jew must have more cash squirreled away somewhere*—and Isaac, finally getting it through his head that however beautiful or even practical his projects, they would always come to nothing in that place, found it prudent to leave town.

He took his family and went up to the land of Palestine: his mother, Tsivia Schnitz; his four children from his first marriage to Nechama-Belinka, who'd gone mad and was put away in an asylum; his second wife, Sarah-Feige, known to all as Mumeh; and the three children he'd had with her. He had a new scheme: oranges. Labor-Zionism had been all the rage among forward-thinking Jews in Belarus, and Isaac had a cousin who'd gone off to drain the swamps in the Galilee.

My grandmother Rose was herself an avid Labor-Zionist all her life and met my grandfather, who was also dedicated to the movement, in Detroit, at the big Poele Zion picnics on Belle Isle. Their photograph albums are full of sepia portraits of the Buffalo, New York, chapter that they joined later, when they moved there, everyone lined up in rows and smiling for the camera, Norma and my father sitting in front on the floor holding a banner, little mascots. My grandfather kept the account books, while my grandmother thrust her blue-and-white *pushke,* charity-box, at all and sundry. She asked for pennies at the bus stop, the grocery store. She raised so much money that she received an award: a brass vase made from a World War I artillery shell by the Jewish craftspeople in Jerusalem. It was the second prize, hideous, but she kept it. The first prize, the one my grandmother had longed for, had been a trip to *Eretz Yisroel,* the land of Israel.

(A few years ago I visited Norma, and in the midst of our conversation she said, "I want you to have something," and produced the artillery shell from her bedroom, where she'd been using it as a doorstop. So now it's an heirloom; useless, it drifts from one spot in my house to another, collecting dust.)

In the mid-1960s, when my grandfather retired, my grandparents finally achieved their lifelong dream and traveled to Israel. Despite their age, they didn't hesitate to settle in a new country, learn a new language: *nu,* they'd done it before. They signed up for intensive Hebrew classes at an *ulpan* and rented an apartment in Hulon, where they lived off and on for many years and became quite popular residents, my grandmother giving everybody what-for in slapdash Hebrew/Yiddish/Russian,

lies about my family

A treasured family artifact: Golda Meier (center) with Rose Hoffman (right) and Morris Hoffman (left). When Golda traveled around the United States promoting Zionism, she stayed at the Hoffman home in Buffalo, N.Y.

while my grandfather carefully placed word beside grammatical word and supplied vocabulary to my grandmother when asked. "Morris," she'd snap her fingers. "Morris, what's, what's . . . in Hebrew, *vi zogt men*?" How do you say?

But in 1899 the family made it only as far as Cyprus, where they were stuck for years, as Ottoman policies about Jewish immigration went this way and that. No foreign Jews to settle in Palestine. Okay, Jewish pilgrims can visit, but no Jewish businessmen. No purchasing of land by foreign Jews. Tsivia died and they buried her there. Sarah-Feige had another child, Sam. Rose learned Greek. Then the Ottomans decided: foreign Jews can buy land in northern Palestine, but not in Jerusalem. Isaac thought he'd finally gotten his chance, but his cousin wrote him a letter advising him to turn around. The Zionists were dying of malaria. The land was either desert or swamp. The Arabs were hostile. And what was it with him and oranges? Trees would take years to mature. How did he think he would live until then?

Malaria they'd already had in Cyprus, not to mention crop failures. Isaac decided to take his cousin's advice.

On November 18, 1912, at the age of forty-two, Isaac Madorsky and his eleven-year-old son Louie sailed on the SS *Kaiser Franz Josef I* from Patras, Greece, to New York City, arriving on December 3: I find the record of their trip on the Ellis Island website. Also traveling with them, according to the ship manifest, was a young lady, twenty-three years old, Dreiza Madorsky, whom neither my aunt nor my father can identify, so the only traces left to history of Dreiza—cousin? maid? fellow villager from Rogachov?—are the particulars, true or false, that she told to the immigration officer. Isaac listed his occupation, wishfully, as "farmer" and claimed never to have been in prison—although there was that time in Russia for forging passports—and not to be a polygamist, despite some ambiguity about the status of poor Nechama-Belinka. He and Louie were just passing through the United States—nonimmigrant aliens who planned to join a cousin in Toronto: profession, professor! Or so Isaac claimed.

On April 3, 1913, the rest of the family boarded the SS *Oceania* in Patras: Sara-Feige, 31; Rosa, 17; Hinda (Jenny), 9; Ber, 5; Dovid, 3; Michel (Max), 2; and Samuel, 6 months. They were headed for Toronto and Isaac, husband and father, at 443 Adelaide Street. The trip was ghastly. When the ship docked at Ellis Island on April 18, the babies were ill with scarlet fever, and the whole group was transported to the quarantine hospital on Hoffman Island in New York harbor, an overcrowded hellhole worse than steerage itself. A few years before, Mrs. Freida Alexandrowski had testified about the conditions there to a reporter for the *New York Times:* sadistic nurses, she said, tied the babies to their cribs and sometimes even gagged them to keep them from crying. During the day, they wheeled them outside in the cold. Many children became sick with multiple illnesses. They might arrive with scarlet fever but then acquire measles and pneumonia, because they were all washed with the same water. The adult dormitories, too, were pestilential, never cleaned or fumigated. Mrs. Alexandrowski said the nurses forced her to scrub floors for twelve hours a day before they'd allow her to see her baby.

Dovid died on April 26. Ber died also, perhaps after the family was released from quarantine on May 2, since Mr. J. H. Hubbenborst, Inspector, did not record his death on the manifest—but maybe he just forgot. My father says both babies are buried on Hoffman Island.

As he and I study the manifest, my father says, "Wait a minute. Where's Alec? What about my Uncle Alec?" Nechama-Belinka had four children, he enumerates: Rose, Alec, Louie, and Jennie. To try to satisfy him, I return to the computer and look through pages and pages of manifests, but neither Alec nor anyone even vaguely answering his description is anywhere to be found, not on the *Kaiser Franz-Joseph* with his father Isaac and brother Louie, not on the *Oceania* with his mother Sara-Feige and his sisters and step-brothers, and not anywhere else.

According to my father, whose memory for numbers is uncanny, Alec was born in 1896 and would have been seventeen. On the manifest, it's Rose who's listed as seventeen, but she was a chronic liar about her age, to the extent of erasing her birth year from every document she owned, mutilating even her treasured diploma from Russian *gymnasium*—high school—and hiding it in a Hebrew-English dictionary, in which, trying to complete an assignment for Sunday school, I found it one afternoon. She was probably born in 1892, my father theorizes, which would have made her twenty-one when she arrived in America, not seventeen. She wasn't married, either, although the manifest lists her that way.

Frustrated with me because I can't account for these contradictions and paradoxes, my father impulsively calls his cousin Arnold, Alec's son, only to be told that Arnold died fifteen years ago. After some confusion and elderly hard-of-hearing shouting, Dad manages to explain to Shirley, Arnold's widow, who he is, and they settle into a long, friendly conversation, at the end of which, both being up-to-date people, they exchange e-mail addresses. I'm glad to have effected this reunion, but we'll never know how Alec got here, or solve the mystery of Dreiza.

I spin a theory: Alec was on the *Oceania* with Sara-Feige and the other children, but he escaped quarantine and made his way alone to his father and brother in Toronto. Eventually, the rest of the family joined them there. Reunited, they crossed the border from Windsor, Ontario, to Detroit, where they had relatives. This much is fact: Isaac, still yearning for a building, bought a hotel in the hot-springs resort of Mount Clemens, Michigan. My father worked there every summer when he was growing up, starting as a dishwasher and eventually becoming a bellhop. Both he and Norma remember their grandfather as a gruff, unfriendly presence, sitting on the porch with the other men, smoking cigars, playing pinochle, watching the action.

"So you didn't like your grandfather," I say to my father.

"No, no, no," he says. "No, no. We just didn't know how to approach him."

In Mount Clemens, Mumeh had three more children: Tsivia (Sylvia), Morris, and Bessie. She kept the hotel going, hugging babies between bouts of rolling out strudel in the kitchen. A big woman, my father says.

# a precious family artifact

*the tape*

My father's grandfather on his father's side was Baruch-Mordechai Zaetz, the *Zayde mitn bord,* the grandfather with a beard; his grandfather on his mother's side was Isaac Madorsky, the *Zayde ohne bord,* the grandfather without a beard. My brother David was named for Baruch-Mordechai, so even now if you ask him what his middle initial M stands for, he says, "Mind-your-own-business."

In my opinion, he should be grateful that Baruch, at least, is only his Hebrew name, and that in English he's David, and not Barry, like one of the college students to whom my parents rented our finished attic one year, for a little extra money. Larry and Barry—Laurence and Baurence, we called them, because what does Barry stand for, anyway? They were Jewish boys, away from home, and my mother invited them to our Passover seder. That year, she served peas for the spring holiday, a little change from her usual asparagus boiled in the pressure cooker, and poor Barry, trying to make conversation, said, "They should make a plate with a wall around it, don't you think? For peas." Sixteen years old, I blurted, "They do. It's called a bowl." I meant nothing by it, but humiliated, Barry and Larry moved out a few weeks later, at the end of the semester, and that was it for boarders. I wasn't blamed, because after all, he'd left himself wide open.

For the stories of these grandfathers, we can thank my Aunt

The *Zayde mitn bord* and his grandchildren, my father, Sigmund (left), and my aunt Norma.

The *Zayde ohne bord*.

Norma, who in around 1968 interviewed her parents on tape, just as, in turn, I interviewed Norma forty years later. My grandmother had just begun to lose her mind to Alzheimer's. The doctors would quiz her, to assess her state of health: "What is today's date? Who is the president of the United States?"

"A *chalyereh*," she groaned.

Gibberish, they noted. Such an intelligent woman. How sad. But in fact, in the case of the political question, at least, she knew exactly what she was talking about: a cholera, a plague. Richard Nixon. My grandparents voted the straight socialist ticket all their lives, except for Franklin Roosevelt.

(This, at least is my father's version of the story. According to his sister Norma, my grandmother did not say "a *chalyereh*" at all. She said, "a *paskudnyak*," a no-good. And furthermore, says Norma, she should know, because she was right there, at her mother's side, while my father was as usual somewhere else.)

The tape begins with Norma saying, "Speak in English," because my grandmother is having a Yiddish conversation in the background.

So my grandmother says, "Yesterday or so it was on the radio a whole sentence in French, and I understood and felt very proud of myself."

"You're very good," says Norma. "You're a linguist." She sounds impatient at this digression, although my grandmother's accomplishments were indeed admirable. She was fluent in Yiddish, Russian, French, and English. She learned some Greek during the family's sojourn on Cyprus, and in her sixties, when my grandfather retired and they moved to Israel for a time, she studied Hebrew. During my stormy Russian period, in high school, when she saw me with my nose in *Crime and Punishment*, she waved at me dismissively. "This I read in Russian. It's much better that way." I picked up Isaac Bashevis Singer instead, but she had no respect for the Jewish Nobelist. "Sex, *dybbuks*. *Bubbemyses*." Ignorant, superstitious nonsense.

"Tell the story, the way your father was arrested," says my grandfather.

"My father was a *starste*," my grandmother immediately complies. "A *starste*, it means an elder."

"A mayor, a mayor," my grandfather corrects her.

"Not a mayor," says my grandmother. "An elder. It's a different thing, *nu*? So he was for ten years a *starste*. And he was a very respected fellow, and that's why every three years they voted for him. They trusted him."

"This was in the village, in Mogilov," says Norma.

"In Rogachov," my grandmother corrects her. "One night come a couple of gentlemen, and take him—to jail! 'Why? Why? Why? What did I do?' 'Never mind! Don't ask why!' *Gendarmeria*."

"Secret service," my grandfather explains.

"Just so," agrees my grandmother. "My father said, 'Could you tell us what we are here for?' And the policeman said, 'You know! Never mind! You know!' And my mother, my stepmother, had a new baby but she was already working. Not working, but busy in the house, with housework, and she also had to replenish the work that had to be done in the store, because she held a store, right in front of our house. And every two days she'd run to Bobroisk."

"Why did she go to Bobroisk?" asks Norma.

"Rogachov, not Bobroisk," says my grandfather.

"Bobroisk, Rogachov," says my grandmother. "My father was a political prisoner, so he was allowed privileges."

In other words, the stepmother was allowed to bring him baskets of food.

"One day, I was playing outside with my brothers and sisters, and we saw Lapin walking in the middle of the street. That was his name, Lapin. He was arrested with my father, but my father is not to be seen, so I got scared. I walked up to Lapin, and I said, 'Please Mr. Lapin, tell me, where is my father?' He says, 'I don't know. They came and took me.' He was a very plain fellow, a dumb Russian. My stepmother kept writing letters to the *gendarmeria,* asking them to release my father. Finally she said to them, 'All right, do! Look at your criminal records and let's see.'"

"But what was he accused of?" asks Norma.

"*Nu,* he was accused," says my grandmother triumphantly. "Up to now, I don't know, so how can you know?"

"Someone must have made something up about him," Norma suggests.

The story threatens to deteriorate into something like the "amusing" tale of Rabbi José, in our Passover Haggadah. Around the seder table, we take turns reading, and this passage always seems to fall to my brother David. Rabbi José loved the holiday so much that he stayed up all night, chanting the blessings and telling the story of the Exodus. In the morning, his students called him, saying, "It's time to recite the morning prayer." We explode in laughter, because the story isn't amusing at all, it's totally pointless. And who ever heard of a Talmudist named José?

Then my grandfather speaks up. "*I* know," he says.

"They kept him and kept him," says my grandmother, ignoring him.

"There are blanks of passports," my grandfather explains. "And those blanks are under a lock. One day, they arrest a few with false passports. And they find out that those blanks come from Rogachov. You see, they suspected that he gave them the passports. And—he did!"

"How do you know this?" says my grandmother.

My grandfather continues, "Even in the old Russia they have a different way of investigating, more civilized than the Communists—with the Communists, they take you to the wall and that's it."

In other words, he means, they shoot you.

"In the old Russia," he continues, "they investigate,

investigate. But they couldn't find that proof. So, they let him out."

"Zalman Madorsky told me that when he wanted to go to America, he came to your father, and your father made him a passport," Norma admits.

"That's right!" says my grandfather.

"Max Madorsky too," my grandmother concedes. "*Nu, ober das ist a gonif?*" That makes him a thief?

So it comes out: my great-grandfather was a forger. Everyone seems to agree that this was hardly a crime but rather a useful skill to have in the family.

"Daddy, now you tell me about your history," says Norma.

"Him?" says my grandmother, being obnoxious. "He has no history!"

He ignores her and says to Norma, "All right, but Mother shouldn't interfere." Never mind that he was interrupting the whole time she was telling her story.

"If she does, she does," says Norma.

My grandfather speaks slowly and deliberately, placing definitive periods at the ends of his sentences, when he pauses to gather his thoughts, perhaps, or to translate, or simply to adjust his false teeth. His stories have a unifying theme: his father's beard.

"Once," he begins, "there was an accident. Two girls were waiting for a streetcar, and at the time there were no platforms, because the streetcar was on rails. So the streetcar came down—and killed them!"

"Ach!" says my grandmother. "Terrible! I never heard of this."

"This happened when my father came six months," says my grandfather. "In Detroit. And the girls were from the richest Jewish family. Naturally, my father used to go to the synagogue every day. And when the two girls were killed, the family notified the *shames*, the caretaker, from the shul, that they needed some men—"

"For a *kaddish*," says Norma.

"Not a *kaddish*," says my grandfather. "To watch the dead. At the time, there were no funeral parlors."

In those first hours, the soul may still be floating around, needing reassurance, so it's a terrific good deed to watch and to comfort the bereaved.

"They took my father, you see, and another few Jews with beards, and when the family saw all those men with beards, they start to"—here my grandfather pauses dramatically and emphasizes the next word as though his listeners may not understand it—"*cry!* You see."

"Two girls, all at once," sighs my grandmother.

"My father said, if he had known, he would never have went."

"He couldn't take it," explains Norma.

"He couldn't take it," my grandfather agrees. "That's one occasion."

In Russia, the *Zayde mitn bord* was a butcher, and when he arrived in Detroit, he took up his old profession. "Imagine a man of fifty-five or sixty starting a business all over again," says Norma.

"Yes, but I should have let him work for someone else for a while to find out," says my grandfather. "So he would see how do they do it here. In the old country they used an axe, you see. They never heard of a saw.

"Here is his butcher store," my grandfather says, "and in the back of the butcher store are rooms, where he lived. And my father liked to drink tea when the water was singing, like in a teakettle, but from a samovar. It's a different taste. So I went and got a piece of pipe, you know, and some charcoal, and took the samovar on the sidewalk. Meanwhile, my father was in the butcher store, with his long *tallis* and his *tfillin* for the morning prayer. That was the way. It took him about an hour and a half until he got through with that prayer."

As the *Zayde* prayed, the samovar would boil and steam, and the customers would look in and leave, or wait. "One Monday morning," says my grandfather, "two Irishmen came to deliver the meat. And there is my father, with the *tfillin,* with the long *tallis,* with the samovar boiling. And the Irishman walks in and sees him—and he faints!"

Clop! Right on the floor. Everyone laughs. "An apparition!" says Norma.

The deliveryman must have thought the *Zayde,* with his beautiful beard and his white prayer-shawl streaming down his back like wings, was an angel of God, descended from heaven in a cloud. Or a devil from Hell, with the *tfillin* on his forehead like a horn, noxious gases steaming around him, and somewhere close by, the axe.

"In 1913," says my grandfather, "I bought a bicycle, to deliver orders." I recognize the way he starts his stories with a date; my father does exactly the same thing, and I used to think I would too, when I grew up. No such luck, my memory doesn't work that way.

"But weren't you going to school then? Or working?" says Norma.

"Working," he says. "Downtown, right on Hastings. So? I was getting up a little earlier."

That summer it was very hot. "There were no refrigerators at that time," says my grandfather. "They would store a lot of ice in the icebox and then keep the meat there. But there wasn't enough ice to supply everybody. There was a scarcity of ice."

(My father has told me a different version of this story. He says the problem was a truckers' strike. There was plenty of ice, just no one to deliver it.)

"So," says my grandfather. "They told my father that the company which supplied coal in the wintertime and ice in summertime was in Jewish hands. They advised my father, he should go down to the office and see the president and beg him, he should give him some ice. So I went with him to the main office, and the minute I walked in with my father, and the president saw his beard—"

"He had a nice beard," says my grandmother.

"He says, 'What does he want?' So, I told him: 'He has meat in the icebox, but if he has no ice, he has to throw it out. What should he do?' The president says, 'Tell Mr. Baruch-Mordechai that before he comes home, the icebox will be full with ice!' And a sure thing," says my grandfather. "We took the bus and came home, and he had called a special truck to deliver the ice."

(A scab truck! It's a good thing my grandfather doesn't know this version of the story.)

"That's another occasion," he says.

"What about your mother?" asks Norma. "Tell us about her."

"In the old country," says my grandfather right away—he's enjoying this, being listened to, instructing—"The butcher goes out and buys a live cattle. He tries to guess the weight, and so on, and he brings it to the slaughterhouse. And when they kill the cattle, you see, they have to examine it, whether it's kosher. They used to take out the lung, blow it up, and see if everything is clean. If the cow or steer is kosher, then you can sell it to the Jewish people. But what happens if you kill a steer, and the *shochet* says, 'It is *treyf*'? The difference in price between kosher and *treyf* is a big one. And in the wintertime, the gentiles don't eat any meat, before their Easter, for six weeks or so. So he loses the money, because there is no market for it, you see.

"So it happened that my father was sitting in the saloon or someplace, drinking a glass of tea, when the mother found out that the cattle he had bought and had killed was *treyf*. And it was in the middle of the winter. So she came over to break the bad news that the ox was *treyf*: 'Ay yay yay yay yay!'"

But what could he do? *Treyf* is *treyf*. A butcher's life is a gamble, and it's the lot of women to worry about the things of this world. The *Zayde* sipped his tea. The mother was furious.

"Things were different in the old country," says Norma.

"Some things," says my grandmother.

The last occasion: Like every kosher butcher, the *Zayde* displayed a Hebrew sign in his shop window: Kosher Meat. The *mashgiach,* who inspected the shop and certified its ritual purity and the *Zayde's* correct observance of religious law, provided the sign, for which the *Zayde* paid fifty cents a week. But one day, says my grandfather, the *mashgiach's* men came and said, "Next week you'll pay us 75 cents. 'And why?' asked the *Zayde.* 'What additional are you providing?' '75 cents.' 'And what will be if I don't pay this?' 'We take the sign!'"

When the *Zayde* heard that, says my grandfather, "He goes to the window, takes out the sign, and says, 'Go, have them take it!' 'What? You can't do business without a sign.' 'Take the sign. I am not afraid for my customers. This beard is my sign!'"

"Ha!" says my grandmother. She quotes the *Zayde:* "'*Mein bord es mein* sign!'"

"You know," adds my grandfather, "chauffeurs, with Catholics, used to come to my father and get the meat because they knew his meat was good. And believe it or not, after the First World War he was making money, because the wholesale price on meat fell very low, but they were charging high prices."

"Very high prices," says my grandmother. "Eggs for ten cents apiece, I remember."

"My mother filled up a basin with water, bought fish, and she was selling fish."

"Fish in the butcher shop?" asks Norma.

"Yes," says my grandfather. "But then the *Forvertz* came out to complain that the butchers were making money."

The *Jewish Daily Forward,* all the way from New York. Even though the *Forvertz* was the socialist paper, it wasn't the one my grandparents read. They thought the Yiddish in it was low class and took the liberal *Tog* instead. Years later, when my parents married, this newspaper preference gave my father's parents something to talk about with my mother's, who also took the *Tog*.

"One woman would come and ask for a pound of meat, she just needed it for a soup, and my father would try to sell her more," says my grandfather. The *Zayde* knew she had the money. "But when another tried to come and buy five pounds, six pounds, he did just the *rewerse*." (Every once in a while there's a consonant that he just can't get his mouth around.) "She had boarders, she had to feed them, she was a poor woman. He used to give her a lot of dog's meat."

So the *Zayde* wasn't such a great, generous Jew after all, even with that righteous beard.

"What prejudice!" says Norma.

"*Ach,* we try to remember our green days," says my grandmother, and with that, the tape runs out.

# the draft

The men in my family don't tell war stories, they tell draft-evasion stories.

At the age of eighteen, my father's father, then called Moishe Zeitz, fled to America to escape conscription into the czar's army—nothing unusual there, so did my mother's father and innumerable Jewish grandfathers all over this country, because even if the Jewish draftees were lucky enough to survive bodily, they lost their souls. In the army, they couldn't pray or study or celebrate the holidays; they couldn't eat kosher food. So many sins, over so many years—for the Jewish soldiers there were no furloughs or discharges. Once they belonged to the czar, he had them through the end of his never-ending wars. Gradually, they forgot their mothers and fathers, forgot their traditions and the holy tongue, forgot their villages, until barely a spark was left of the boys they once had been.

The sons taken as soldiers, the daughters raped, the babies bayoneted, the mamas and papas burned alive in their houses: this is how the Russians destroyed the Jewish family, and we mourn those generations, chanting *Kol Nidre* on Yom Kippur to remember, among other tragedies, their soldierly vows—the duress under which they were taken, the irresistible pull of the life force dragging them to lie—even now, after the great Destruction, when the Jews of my grandfather's town of Mosyr, the remnant left after years of pogroms, war, and emigration, were force-marched to the bank of the Pripyat River, where they had once fished and picnicked, there to be shot and stomped and drowned. Already contaminated by the murdered Jews, the Pripyat, which flows past Chernobyl, is now irredeemably polluted.

But roll the calendar back before all that. My great-grandfather, Baruch-Mordechai Zeitz, was conscripted but survived to return home. The story is in a little memoir my grandfather wrote just before he died, and here it is in his words, helpfully translated from the Yiddish by his daughter, my Aunt Norma:

My father was born in 1854. When Alexander the Second instituted the draft of twenty-year-olds, my father was taken as a soldier. He was already married. He served in Bobroisk, a fortress that dates back to Napoleon's time. They taught him to be a musician.

He and a few other Jewish soldiers were religious, and they did not want to eat nonkosher meat. One Shabbat, they went to the synagogue in town, and when it came time to take out the Torahs for the reading of the week, they all went up on the *bima* and wouldn't let them continue with the service. The rabbi listened to their plea: they did not want to eat the army's unclean food.

The rabbi thought a bit and said, "You may eat it. You are in the army."

The soldiers answered, "Very good, Rabbi. You taste the first spoonful from the pot. Then we will eat."

A tumult broke out in the synagogue, but finally the soldiers were promised that kosher food would be provided for them. It was arranged that their officer was paid, and they ate what the Jewish community had prepared for them.

The Russo-Turkish War broke out. My father gave my mother a pseudodivorce and went to war. They encircled Plevna. My father was in the field barracks. He made a small fire, and by the light of the fire, he began to say his prayers. A shell from the enemy fell near the fire. My father quickly put the fire out and retreated.

Russia advanced into Turkey and occupied some of the towns. The Jewish soldiers decided to visit the local synagogue. Everyone there wanted to have them as their guests for Shabbat.

The war ended, and he came home in peace. This was in the year 1877.

Let me call your attention to several notable details in this story. First, that rabbi. The Lubavitcher hasidim, who have a million websites all over the Internet, in the hope of bringing us apostate Jews back to fold, heap praise on their holy Rabbi Hillel, who provided kosher food for the Jewish soldiers of the Bobroisk fortress—but they say nothing of the soldiers' challenge to the rabbi, nor of the *shabbes* riot that led the community to undertake this *mitzvah*. And neither my grandfather nor the Lubavitchers has recorded anything about how the overburdened community solved the problem of raising enough money to bribe the mess officer, not to mention pay the expense of all those extra meals.

Second, the pseudodivorce. As is traditional, at least among forward-thinking and considerate men, my great-grandfather divorced his wife before going to war so that if, God forbid, he went missing in action, she would not be left for years in a state of ambiguous widowhood, but could remarry.

Third, the small fire and the retreat. Baruch-Mordechai, though exemplary in his religious observance, was clearly a pragmatist. Unwilling to risk his life for God or czar, he knew when to douse the fire and run.

Fourth, the Jews of Turkey. They instantly and correctly recognized the Jewish soldiers, with their propensity to retreat, as their brothers rather than as the Russian enemy.

Luck like Baruch-Mordechai's, though, can't be counted on, and in 1907 his son, my grandfather, departed Mosyr for America, to join his older sister Gittel, who had left in a big hurry a couple of years before, during the 1905 Revolution, amid rumors that out in the cowshed she was making a bomb, to blow up the local mayor. (Or was it Yossel, her boyfriend, eventually my great-uncle, who was making the bomb? Was there a bomb at all? My father tells the story in various versions. In one, Gittel meets Yossel only when she comes to America. Then my father shows me a photograph, taken in Europe, in which both of them appear. Apparently. But who can really tell one dressed-up blur of villagers, in their braids and kerchiefs, beards and hats, from another?) When my grandfather stepped off the boat in New York, he encountered a band playing festive music to welcome the new arrivals—what a country! Well, actually, he learned, the band was welcoming the American president, William Howard Taft, who had come to observe the immigrants—okay, that's not so bad either!

At least, that's the story my grandfather told. He said he came through Castle Garden, an immigration center near Ellis Island but smaller and less famous. And why doubt him? Throughout his life he was known for being accurate to a fault. He worked as a draftsman, a job requiring concentration and meticulous attention to detail. When he spoke, it was slowly, as he weighed the correctness of each word. Nevertheless, Castle Garden has no record of anyone with his name or anything like it coming through in 1907; in fact, all the ships arriving there in that year were Italian. And the president? Theodore Roosevelt. Taft was elected in 1908, inaugurated in 1909.

Of course, these glitches are easily explained. The immigration records of the time are notoriously full of errors and gaps. The ship manifests list whatever information the passengers felt like supplying about their names, marital status, villages of origin, amount of money in their pockets, criminal records, anarchist tendencies—in the New World, everything became new. Maybe my grandfather made up a name to give the immigration officer, as he was to do later, under similar circumstances. After all, the absence of a record doesn't mean he didn't exist. I saw him, with my own eyes, many times, in this country. And maybe my grandfather saw candidate Taft. Or President Roosevelt. Or for once got a date mixed up.

From Castle Garden he went to Gittel in Detroit, where he had ten good years. The study habits he had learned in *cheder* enabled him to ace American high school at night, in a year. He found a job, brought his parents over from Mosyr, and set up Baruch-Mordechai in a butcher shop, just like in the old country. His free time he devoted to teaching in the *Yiddishe Folkschule* and working with the *Poale Zion,* where he met other like-minded people. He raised money for the Jews in the Holy Land, he attended lectures, he sang the songs of the Jewish pioneers and danced the *hora*—can I imagine my dignified grandfather in his suit and tie hopping up and down and kicking his feet? No, but that's what the young Zionists did in those days, and he did whatever was necessary for the cause. On one of the group's Sunday picnics at Belle Isle park, he met my grandmother, Rose Madorsky.

This peaceful life ended in 1917, when the United States entered the Great War and instituted a draft. My grandfather ran away to Canada so precipitously that, like the Israelites who fled into the desert to escape the pharoah's army, he carried nothing with him, not even a piece of bread or a change of

My grandparents, Morris Hoffman and Rose (Madorsky) Hoffman.

clothes. A few days later, Rose followed with his possessions, and they stayed in Toronto for two years, until the end of the war. Then, they wanted to return to the states and their families. My grandfather, afraid of being caught, changed his name officially from Zeitz to Hoffman, claiming to the Canadian judge who presided over the process that his wife disdained his ridiculous name, which, he said, means "rabbit" in Russian. (Peasants and Jews in Russia had had only first names and patronymics until the mid-nineteenth century, when the czar ordered them to take last names, and many, especially the peasants, were saddled with their village nicknames: Squinty, Stinky, Rabbit-Ears. Requests for changes were not uncommon.) My Aunt Norma, who was born during her parents' sojourn in Toronto, which caused a brief panic over her citizenship later on, still has the document that dubbed Moshe Zeitz "Morris Hoffman."

During the terrible years of the Vietnam War, when boys were again fleeing to Canada to escape the draft, my father occasionally threatened over dinner to move our whole family there too—or what about to Israel? In Israel we'd all have to go into the army, even the girls, but at least there we'd be fighting for the Jews. It was then that my father told us the story of our name, which wasn't ours at all. My grandfather had borrowed it from a friend.

"Ha, ha!" my father says now. "You kids thought your grandpa the draft dodger was pretty cool."

"*Cool?* Daddy, please." He makes it sound ridiculous, but he's right. I do think it's cool to have a heritage of radical thought and action. I'm proud of what my grandfather did, even if it was out of fear or cynicism rather than, as I'd wish, pacifist principle, and proud that my grandparents were Labor-Zionists who voted socialist all their lives except, of course, for Franklin Roosevelt. I love the fact that my grandmother forbid my father to join the Boy Scouts because she thought they were a bunch of fascists—"And she was right!" my father says. I'm proud even of my liberal parents, who were abused as communists in the local newspaper whenever they stuck their necks out, to serve on the town's civil rights commission or to campaign against prayer in the schools—a particular cause of my mother's, after I came home from kindergarten reciting the Our Father and singing my favorite song, "Silent Night."

My grandfather, though, was far from proud of his draft dodging and the deceptions it necessitated. It haunted him all his life, so much so that when the United States entered World War II, he developed an ulcer, unable to shake the notion that his boss would discover his evasion of service during the previous war and cut back to zero the one day per week of work to which he'd managed to cling throughout the Depression. He decided to come clean and asked the man for an appointment to discuss a grave personal matter. Trembling, he explained his situation.

"And I'm supposed to do something about this?" said his boss. "Don't bother me with this nonsense."

Back at his drawing board, my grandfather's mood began to lift, and Norma says that from then on, he was a changed person, lighter, happier—although the ulcer lingered. When he and my grandmother came to stay with us in the Berkshires during the summer, my mother would soft-boil an egg for his breakfast.

My grandfather was too old, of course, to serve in World War II, the "just war," but not my father, although he's never given any hint that he was eager to sign up. He talks more often about escape. When my mother turns away his desire to buy her rings and necklaces, he lectures her: "Jews have always had diamonds. We can sew them into our coats if we need to flee."

"Flee?" I defend my mother. "What do you think, we're back in Russia?"

"You're like the Jews in Germany," he says. "Assimilated."

On this subject he's insane. At least my mother still has no significant jewelry.

A college student, functionally blind without his glasses, he reported to his draft board in 1942, when the government lowered the draft age from twenty-one to twenty, but he was rejected because of his terrible vision. In 1944 the age was lowered again, to eighteen, and so were the standards. His eyesight was no longer a barrier. My grandfather accompanied him to his physical, kissed him, and said, "If only I could go in your place, my son."

During basic training, my father was given an aptitude test. Pass, and he'd be sent to Yale to learn Japanese; fail, and he'd be sent overseas with the infantry. So, he says, he did his best to pass. What luck! He enjoyed the language classes, met a bunch of other smart guys with whom he still keeps in touch, and was able to embarrass me throughout my childhood by attempting to speak to the grandparents of my classmate Bobby Hirata, who lived around the corner, in their native tongue—as well as to any Japanese tourists we happened to encounter. The elderly Hiratas mostly laughed when he greeted them, either because they thought a tubby white guy with Coke-bottle glasses should not try to speak Japanese or because the Japanese he'd been taught in the army was archaic and stilted. But the tourists appreciated it, since he is not only very friendly but also can give excellent directions to anyplace you might want to go. In a typical military snafu, however, my father never actually went to Japan. He was sent to Korea, where the locals were more likely to be offended than impressed by a GI's Japanese language skills and who preferred anyway to speak to the soldiers in English, for practice.

In contrast to his surprisingly positive military experience my father cites the example of his friend. "George," he says, "was everywhere. Italy. France. Even now he can't talk about it. Can't watch a war movie. *Saving Private Ryan*? Couldn't watch it. He still has shell shock. Post-traumatic stress. And this is what I don't understand," my father continues. "What makes a man fearless, willing to walk into bullets? How did they do it? I still can't figure it out completely. It has something to do with loyalty to the squad. In basic training, we did everything together."

In my generation we're mostly girls, thank God, although my brother David was of military age during the final years of the Vietnam War. At the lake, we would put Arlo Guthrie's album *Alice's Restaurant* on the record player, and the little kids would dance. The song is about the draft, and how the military had gotten so desperate they'd take students, criminals, anyone: "Mother rapers. Father stabbers. Father rapers!" Arlo raps. His story takes place in Stockbridge, right down the road from Great Barrington, where we were. We knew the policeman who arrested him, and the church his friend Alice had remodeled into a home. We felt a special connection to the popular song.

Back in those days I never wondered what David was thinking as we laughed and danced. At a family gathering a few years ago, surrounded by my enormous hockey-champ nephews, he was reminding me that our parents never went to his high school track meets, even when his team won the state championship, when in that free-associative way he has of suddenly throwing out random information, he veered onto another topic. He informed me that when he drew a low number in the draft lottery, my father had offered to send him to Canada. I'd had no idea.

He was furious about it. "Canada? Me?" To him, the offer was not love and survival but exile, and he wasn't going to start up with that again.

"So what was your plan?" I asked, wondering: Would I have taken my father up on such an offer? Would I have had the guts? Alone, illegal, in a foreign country. My grandfathers' situations exactly.

David ignored my question and continued. "He had no idea. None! Of what I was going through. I watched the lottery with my roommates on TV, and it stopped short of my number. So I was lucky." Then he answered my question: "But I would have served."

And he would have. He is the kind of person who does what needs to be done. His cardinal virtue is loyalty: to family, to employer, to country if it comes to that. He stays in touch with people from our high school, while I can't even remember their names. When I was in my twenties, during the war, I thought this loyalty of his was no virtue at all but rather a terrible flaw. I see it differently now, especially because of course I've got it too. I love him unconditionally.

My brother David is bald and bespectacled. He is smart and mean, the prince of the cutting remark, the kind I laugh at and then hate myself for in the morning. He has no patience and a rotten temper. He thinks he's better than you. Him, in the army? One of the guys? Greeting his buddies with a little punch to the shoulder? Doing pushups? Cutting his way through jungle and swamp? Shooting guns?

My heart seizes. He never would have made it.

# stuffing

My grandmother was known for her cooking. My father remembers her canning fruit all summer—peaches, plums, cherries both sweet and sour. She stored the jars on shelves in the cellar, where they glowed deliciously in the darkness, orange, purple, red.

"She would get soup meat and ask for extra bones. Those were free," his sister, my Aunt Norma, tells me in an e-mail. "The leftover meat she would grind and make meat blintzes. With the chicken she would make soup, then roast the chicken, use the wings and feet for fricassee, and the liver she chopped with chicken fat and hard-boiled eggs and onion. So from one chicken we had several delicious meals."

That's what she wrote: "delicious meals"—not excepting even the fat, the liver, or the feet. "It was the Depression," she adds, and I think that it's a good thing I was born during the prosperous fifties and did not have to endure the hardships of the older generation. I have certain textural aversions; I can't eat even a soft-boiled egg, never mind a scaly, cartilaginous foot. What I remember of my grandmother's cooking is strudel: she would arrive our house with a yeast version rolled with cinnamon, nuts, and raisins. That was okay. But her supreme production, which I always hoped for but which rarely appeared, was apple strudel.

"When *my* mama made strudel she spread a white cloth

over the kitchen table," says my mother. "She stretched and stretched the dough, until you could see through it." Her comment surprises me. Usually when she talks about her mother's cooking, it's about the disgusting folk-cures she forced upon her, to fatten her up and stop her constant coughing: a whole onion, boiled in honey; *p'tchah,* calves' foot jelly with garlic; and the dreaded, slimy *guggle-muggle,* a raw egg cracked into a glass of milk—which my mother in turn forced upon me, although she denies it up and down. I remember the *guggle-muggle* clearly. She made it with chocolate milk, which, believe me, didn't help. Cooking makes my mother anxious—so many people to please and ingredients to assemble, and she herself has never been much of an eater. As a result, she's terrible at it. Yet, you can't tear her away from the stove. She takes it on, like Jesus the sins of the Christians, so others won't suffer.

"Let me make the dinner, Ma," I suggest. "I like cooking." I'm not saying this to persuade her; it's the honest truth. I clip recipes from the newspaper; I subscribe to glossy magazines with pictures of roasts and cakes on the covers. My favorite day of the week is Wednesday, when the *New York Times* publishes its food section, while on Wednesdays my mother complains that there's nothing to read.

"No, no. I already went shopping," she says. "You relax."

I remember clearly that it was my father's mother who baked us apple strudel, not my mother's—even if my father now marvels that she had the patience for such a project. On Passover she fried *chremzls,* matzo-meal pancakes, light and crispy, just for my mother, who adored them and who had been my grandmother's favorite from the moment they met. My father loves to tell the story of bringing her home to introduce her to his parents. After dinner, when my mother had disappeared into the kitchen to help out with the dishes, my grandmother pulled him to her and whispered loudly—was there any other way to whisper?—"She's too good for you."

I fly to Florida to interview Norma about our family history, of which she is the guardian. She constructed a family tree that goes back to the eighteenth century, tape-recorded the older generation, and gathered photographs and other odds and ends. She displays my great-grandfather's samovar in her living room. "Later I'll tell you about the samovar," she promises.

"What about it?" I ask.

"Not now," she says.

I set up my tape recorder, and she begins without my having to ask her a thing: her earliest memory is of her mother chasing her around the kitchen table with a spoon. As a child, she wouldn't eat. "Funny thing," she says. "I was never hungry."

When her mother caught her and pushed her down into a chair, Norma clenched her teeth. The spoon knocked at her lips. Suddenly, her mother pointed. "*Vos is dos?*"

Sullen. "What? The window." In slipped the spoon.

"*Yiddish! Red Yiddish in hois!*" For speaking English at home, Norma usually got a slap.

Obediently: "*Fenster.*" Another mouthful.

Quickly wise to that, the child held the food in her cheeks, refusing to swallow, and her mother, furious at being proved less stubborn than her daughter, had to let her go. After one of these battles, her mother decided, "Okay, forget it, when you get hungry, you'll come to me."

"That was the happiest day of my life," says Norma.

The skirmish lost, the war raged on. Norma started school, and a doctor appeared in her class to weigh and measure all the children. He reported back to her mother: Norma was underweight. Underweight! A red flag to a bull. Now every day her mother gave her a big sandwich, to eat during recess. Peanut butter, cream cheese, jam. No one else had sandwiches. Norma hid them in her desk. She gave them to the Delgati kids from upstairs, and Mrs. Delgati, watching from the window, saw the exchange and tattled to Norma's mother.

"How was the sandwich, darling?" her mother asked sweetly, when Norma came home from school, setting the trap.

"Delicious," said Norma, "but please, no more—"

"Delicious, hah!" Her mother pounced.

"Did I get a verbal beating!" Norma tells me. "My mother called me all kinds of names. I was a liar, and she was going to tell everybody, and everybody's going to know I'm a liar. And I thought, 'Ah, if only I could just go through the floor.' I thought, 'Maybe when I'm older it won't hurt so much and I'll laugh.' Well, here I am. I'm old. It was terrible and I'm still not laughing." And she laughs, brief and bitter.

Each day when Norma came home from school, she would rush outside to play with her friends. But this peaceful interval never lasted long. Her mother would call her inside, thrust a book into her hand, point to the place where they'd left off the day before. "*Laynen zich.*" Read.

Norma read aloud in Yiddish while her mother ironed, or sewed, or cooked, or rushed back and forth from one to the other. She could never stick to any single activity for very long, and even things like eating dinner or reading Russian novels, which a normal person does sitting still, she did on the fly—a taste from the pot, a coin of salami, a *nosh*, the book open before her on the table. "She'd kneel on a kitchen chair, with one knee, like she was ready to do something else," says Norma, "and she'd start the book. But right away she wanted to know what was going to happen. So she would go to the end to see how it turned out. But she couldn't understand how they got to that end, so she'd flip back a few pages. And that's how she read—backwards!"

"She got things done because she was fast," my father, usually his mother's champion, later admits to me. "She was completely inefficient and disorganized." He would come home from school for lunch, which she would leave for him on the kitchen table. The front door was never supposed to be locked, but sometimes she forgot. He could see his lunch through the window. "Ma, I had to break in again through the basement," he told her.

"*Nu,* you ate, didn't you?" The thing he hated the most was the bus ticket scam. As a child under the age of twelve, he paid half fare, a penny. His mother would push him out the door to catch the bus, and he would ride to the next stop and request a transfer. Then he would walk back, quickly, not out-and-out guiltily running, glancing behind him, expecting every minute to see the angry bus driver gaining on him. Back at the house, his mother would hold out her hand for the transfer.

One day, Norma came home from school, and when her mother thrust the Yiddish book at her, Norma said, "I can't. I have homework."

"Homework!"

"The teacher says we have to hand it in tomorrow." Norma pulled up a chair to the kitchen table, arranged paper and pencils before her, opened a book, began to scribble and calculate.

The next morning, in the doorway of Norma's classroom, her mother appeared, short and determined, in battle-dress: her good navy shirtwaist, cinched with a black patent-leather belt. Red lipstick, a round hat like a velvet tiara, white gloves. "*Oy,* Mama, what are you doing here?" Norma cried.

Her mother ignored her and marched up to the teacher. "You have her all day," she told her. "When she gets home, she's mine."

It was terrible, realizing at that moment how completely she belonged to her mother and how little recourse she had. The school was complicit. Her intimidated teacher exempted her, among all the children, from homework, which she would gladly have done; she would have enjoyed having a project of her own. The assignments were never difficult.

"Growing up was not easy with a mother who had her own mind," Norma says. "I was very rebellious when I got to be a teenager, and I remember saying, '*Vos shtupst mir azoy fil?*' 'Why are you stuffing me so much?' With culture and things, you know—history."

My father, his parents' dear Sonny, went away to college—he worked night and day, in the cafeteria, on the school farm milking cows, but still he went away, and sent his laundry home in a cardboard suitcase, Norma remembers, until the suitcase fell apart. She meanwhile lived at home and traveled to class on the streetcar, although she longed to go to the state university in Fredonia, where she could have majored in music. She played the piano and the cello. "But the money had to go to Sig, my brother, because he was the man, and he was going to have to earn a living for the family. And I accepted that," she says. "And yet I hear about women who fought it, and I think to myself, Why was I such a lamb?"

Her college years coincided with the Spanish Civil War, and her professors supported the fascists. She had to argue constantly. Exasperated, one of them cut off the conversation: "Miss Hoffman! The trouble with you is that you read too much!"

You can't get an education in a place like that. "I had to fill in afterward," Norma says, and I know just how she feels. In my stupid high school, I was constantly raising my hand and saying, "I disagree—" and my friends would cringe, they told me. There she goes again. Even I could see it only irritated everybody, and I didn't enjoy becoming a spectacle, but I couldn't stop myself. Remaining silent in the presence of wrong is a sin: this had been drummed into me forever, ever since we'd been called to the auditorium in Hebrew elementary school and made to watch *Night and Fog*. Certainly I didn't need to see the posters that appeared everywhere in the late eighties to know that SILENCE = DEATH; I'd taken that in with my mother's milk. (And as a talkative friend of mine said when she heard the slogan, "In that case, we Jews have nothing to worry about.") My teachers couldn't stand me. When the time came to give out prizes, they blackballed me from the National

Honor Society, even though my grades were perfect. Well, *ptui* on them! My whole family is still proud of me for it.

Norma married young, "I guess to get out of the house," she says. Her husband, Gene Lerner, was a pill, everyone says, like it's part of his name: Lerner-That-Pill. I myself never met that fascinating character, the first husband, father of my cousins Ronnie and Elissa, my favorite. The marriage was a mistake. By the time I arrived on the scene, Norma and Gene were divorced, the only divorce on either side of the family until my sister Judith broke up with He-Who-Shall-Not-Be-Named, many years later. "I felt like I was wearing a scarlet letter," Norma says. It was the fifties.

Norma's second husband was Bud Salz, whose real name, we kids used to marvel, was Norman, of all things: Norma and Norman. "That was the real love match," my father tells me—generously, since I know that, in his opinion, Bud was a big know-it-all. He was an engineer and mathematician, and his life's goal, which he eventually achieved, was to solve something called the Traveling-Salesman Problem: given a certain number of cities, say twenty-seven, and certain costs and distances, calculate the cheapest, most direct way to visit each city and return to your starting point. The practical application of the Traveling-Salesman Problem eludes me, since in life costs and distances never turn out as predicted, and personally I think he should have chosen to address instead the classic Aunt Pearl's Dilemma. My mother's sister was faced at one point with twin babies, several bags of groceries, and a third-floor walkup in Queens: so, Mr. Scientist, figure out how to carry babies and groceries up the stairs making the fewest number of trips and leaving each baby alone for the least amount of time.

Norma and Bud had two sons, Simon and Jonah, who were the same ages as my brother David and sister Judy. With the divorces and successive marriages, everyone in that family had networks of siblings, halves and steps; I'd never encountered anything like it. Ronnie sometimes lived with his father, so he wasn't always there when we visited, but sometimes Danny Asimov was—Bud's son from his first marriage, who usually lived with his mother. Elissa said I should consider Danny my *quasi cousin,* since he wasn't really related to me at all, nor to her, for that matter, thus drawing me, too, into the web. Each year when we visited Buffalo—an eight-hour drive from New Jersey, which we kids spent kicking each other and arguing over who got carsick the most and therefore deserved the window seat—my cousins and their various siblings and quasis would be obsessed with a different unusual game: tiddlywinks, backgammon, pogo sticking. Dictionary, in which each player made up a definition for an obscure word like "quasi," whose true meaning no one knew.

Bud's family were Communists. "They signed on in the thirties, to make life better for everyone," says Norma. "They didn't know what we know now." He and his brother and sister were in the Young Communist League, and they would go to Union Square on the weekends, to hear the Communists on their soapboxes perorating on revolution. Bud, being Bud, heckled them. Or at least, that's how the Party saw it. He shouted out questions, he interjected facts that the speakers had conveniently ignored, he proposed alternative interpretations, and after several incidents, the Young Communist League kicked him out.

Twenty years later, Norma and Bud were living in Farmingdale, New York, where Bud was working for the Sylvania company. He had even acquired a patent, for a method of testing camera flashbulbs. Before that, Norma explains proudly, the only way to know for sure whether they would work was to set them off, and of course you couldn't use them after that. Then, it all fell apart. "When McCarthy finished with Hollywood," Norma says, "he came to Long Island." Bud was called in for an interview, in which he was asked to list the people who had come to visit his family during the thirties and forties, and even to implicate his brother and sister, now teaching in the New York City public schools. The fact that he'd made such a poor Communist that the Party had expelled him didn't gain him any mercy from the House Un-American Activities Committee. He told them nothing. His security clearance was revoked, his brother and sister fired.

Sylvania kept him on in an administrative position, for which, Norma says, she and Bud were grateful, but without his security clearance Bud couldn't do much, since all the jobs there were on contract for the government, and after a while the company let him go. The outlook was bleak, with all the various children and no money coming in. Norma and Bud scraped together everything they had, borrowed from their parents, and hired a lawyer, who instructed them to collect affidavits from everyone they knew, "swearing to Bud's . . . Bud's patriotic patriotism," Norma spits out. Some people refused to get involved, like their next-door neighbor, a Hungarian immigrant. But eventually the affidavits worked, or maybe it was just that the times had changed, and McCarthy had fallen. Bud got back his security clearance, and they had a big celebration, for everyone they knew, even the Hungarian, with a sign above the door for all to see: "Clearance Party."

I have to push Norma into telling me this story. Her husband's persecution for being a Communist—or not, as it happens—is perhaps a shameful memory. I'd never heard about it before. Unlike Norma, I'm bursting with pride. In our family we have suffered for our convictions! "This isn't what I want to talk about," Norma says. "I want to tell you the history of our family. For instance, about the samovar."

"Okay," I say. She's ninety years old, I remind myself. She can tell her story however she wants. "What about the samovar?" She leads me into the living room, and we admire it.

"Your great-grandfather brought it from Europe," she says. In it, my grandfather, his son, would make him tea. But when

the great-grandfather died, the samovar went not to my grandfather but to his sister in Detroit. Every summer, my grandmother would visit, and one summer when she left, the samovar disappeared with her.

"My mother didn't really steal it," my father rationalizes,
when I tell him the samovar is in Norma's living room. "She
assumed that since it had been her husband's, it was hers."
Except it wasn't her husband's—it was his father's.

Norma inherited it from her mother, unaware, she claims,
of its dubious provenance. But without my grandfather to set it
up, it no longer whistles and steams. Or maybe after traveling
in the great-grandfather's luggage from Belorus to New York
City to Toronto to Detroit, and then being smuggled somehow
under my grandmother's coat to Buffalo and finally flying with
Norma to Miami, it's broken. One of the Detroit cousins visited
Norma a few years ago and said, "Our samovar!" but Norma
refused to give it up—correctly, says my father. "Those cousins
would have lost it by now."

"See how it's etched all over," Norma shows me. "Beautiful.
It's going to Elissa." Don't get any ideas, she means. Which I
have been. I covet it, the oldest thing our family owns. Norma
turns it over to show me a stamp, the name of a Russian brass
works and the year it was made, sometime in the 1850s. She
places it back on the shelf.

"After McCarthy, Bud found a new job, in Buffalo of all
places," she says when we've resettled ourselves around the
kitchen table. "Simon was four and Jonah was three.

"It took courage to go back, because I had divorced a man
there. My ex-husband had remarried, and we saw him and his
wife at some event, and when she walked by our table, she spat.
She'd make calls to us on the phone and just breathe." The new
wife even called Norma's friends to spread stories about her,
although one, Norma tells me, said, "I'm a friend of Norma's,
and I don't want to hear such stories."

"Only one? But Aunt Norma, that's what they all should have said!"

"It was her purpose to knock me out, completely," Norma continues. Of course, Norma being her mother's daughter, the woman accomplished no such thing.

At ninety, Norma is still banging around Miami, organizing Jewish film festivals and oral-history classes and book-discussion groups, picking up her granddaughter from Hebrew school and me from my hotel. Her hair is bright red, in a short cut she tells me is brand new. "But maybe it's too short?" she asks me. "I think it makes my nose look big."

"Not at all," I say. "It's very stylish." And so it is.

Between activities, we sit in her kitchen with my tape recorder running. "I'm losing my voice with all this talking," she says. She takes me to the weekly Yiddish conversation class she leads at the community college, so she can show me off to the other oldsters, and we pass around a story Norma has photocopied. The group is charmed by my ability to read when my turn comes up. I studied Yiddish in graduate school, and I've known the Hebrew alphabet since kindergarten. Really, though, I'm an ignoramus: I can spell out the words, but I don't understand what they mean.

# communists and socialists and their ambitions

Sol.  In 1900 the Baron DeHirsch Fund established the Jewish Agricultural Society, with the purpose of moving immigrants out of the urban slums and onto the land: "free farmers on their own soil," in the words of the society. Most of the immigrants had never considered living outside the city. In Europe, the Jews were not allowed to own land. The society provided training as well as loans and published an informative Yiddish/English monthly called *The Jewish Farmer,* of all things, the juxtaposition of "Jewish" and "farmer" so incongruous it sounds like a Borsht Belt routine. Although at first the society supported "group colonization," it shifted fairly early to funding individuals. Those who took the deal were idealistic, socialist, and secular, and quickly formed networks and established community centers.

According to a 1987 article in the *New York Times,* New Jersey was a particularly attractive location because it was "close to markets—and relatives" in New York City—although Jewish farmers also set up in Connecticut, New York state, and Petaluma, California. Most got into chickens. With a loan of $2,000 from the Jewish Agricultural Society, says the article, "a family could buy a five-acre farm with a house and chicken coops. When the chicks matured five months later into hens, a farmer was in business. One chicken could bring in $2.00 profit a year, so 2,000 chickens would yield $4,000 a year, a decent living in the early 1950s. In the heyday of Jewish chicken farming, there were twelve hundred of the farms in Lakewood, Farmingdale, and Tom's River, New Jersey."

My Uncle Sol's chicken farm was in Lakewood.

He and my Aunt Jen, my grandmother's youngest sister, moved to the farm from Harlem, where they had run a radio repair shop "on 125th Street and St. Nicholas Avenue," my father e-mails me with typical precision, a couple of blocks from what he characterizes as "the only hotel in NYC that would allow blacks." Sure enough, when I check his information I find that the Hotel Theresa, desegregated in 1940 and known as the Waldorf-Astoria of Harlem, was on 125th and Seventh, next to the Apollo Theater, and entertainers and celebrities like Duke Ellington, Louis Armstrong, and Lena Horne, not to mention Fidel Castro, put up there when they came through town. Sol met them when he fixed their sound systems and other equipment. And, Jen once remarked, smoked marijuana with them. "*Feh,*" she told us when it came back into vogue. "I tried it years ago."

But then, Jen was known for never liking anything, and for saying of anyone else's cooking, particularly her daughter-in-law's, and of her daughter-in-law herself, "I hate it—but I never complain." Her specialty was cinnamon *babka*, baked in a family-sized Maxwell House coffee can for easy freezing. To remove the cake, you just cranked open the bottom of the can and pushed it out. She gave us one whenever we visited— because even though most things had been put on this earth to torment her, my mother was different. Jen adored her.

"So delicious," said my mother. "Thank you, Aunt Jen."

"Some people know what's good," said Jen. The unspoken comparison to her daughter-in-law hung in the air.

But Sol had no need of help from the Jewish Agricultural Society or anyone else. "And all this time I thought he was one of the famous Jewish-socialist chicken farmers of South Jersey," I say to my father. "This is so disappointing."

"Nah, Sol was no socialist," he says. "Sol was a communist!" Maybe even a capital-C Communist: my father doesn't specify whether Sol was a Party member, just that Sol's politics led to terrible arguments with my grandparents about the establishment of the state of Israel. They couldn't have been more strongly in support, while Sol completely opposed it. According to him, if Israel became a state, it would be like any other, waging imperialist wars, exploiting the workers. But what about from each according to his ability, and the *kibbutzim,* and the end of persecution and diaspora? He didn't buy it. That's not the way the world works.

"I'm with Sol," I tell my father. "Look how it turned out."

He pretends his hearing aid is turned off and doesn't answer me.

Sol may have been a communist, but he had certain capitalist talents and impulses. By 1943 he had saved about $12,000 from the radio store, which he decided to invest in a farm where he and Jen could live off the land, mortgage-free. And it worked: they had a beautiful house and five thousand chickens, and they were happy—even Jen was happy. But like the fisherman's wife in the fairy tale, Sol wanted more and ever more. "The original plan was lost in his ambition to grow bigger and better," is how my father puts it in his e-mail to me. Sol bought an apple orchard. Then he hired migrant workers. Then the apples turned out to be of poor quality. Then he lost his shirt. Finally, he went back into chickens, but this time with heavy debt.

The second chicken farm coincided with my early childhood, and both my brother David and I remember the thrill of visiting it. Dogs, chickens, our very tall uncle in khaki work clothes smoking a cigar, our little aunt in the kitchen. David wanted to help gather the eggs but kept crushing them in his fist. By then, though, times had changed for chicken farmers: the

My great-uncle, Sol Shockman.

price of eggs was regulated, says my father, but not the price of feed, which went up and up. The situation was impossible. Farms failed throughout the 1950s, and that was the end of the Jewish-socialist chicken-farming movement.

Sol's son-in-law took him into the toy business, and he and Jen moved to Camden.

"Sol was wonderful, but he reached for the stars too often. His ambition was infinite. I loved him dearly," my father concludes.

Max. Max Madoff was the husband of my grandmother's cousin Sorke, of whom she spoke often. Sorke, Sorke, Sorke— I loved hearing her roll this name around in her mouth. The couple must have been related in some degree when they met, because Madoff is a shortened form of Madorsky, Sorke's maiden name. Growing up I was told that, "Hoffman" being an arbitrary designation my grandfather had picked up to cross the Canadian border, we had no Hoffman relatives: not Abbie, "Revolution is a perpetual process embedded in the human spirit," as I had to explain over and over in the seventies to the people—the FBI?—who'd dialed "A. Hoffman" hoping to raise him on the phone; not Hans, the artist, as I tell the librarian in Provincetown every time I check out a book—he's got one *f* and two *n*'s; and not Joe, who apparently gets his car fixed at the same shop that I do and who my mechanic is convinced is my father. But, my parents said, we were related to all Madorskys, as well as to Madoffs, Madows, Madors, and other derivatives. This turns out to be not quite true. We are not, fortunately, related to Bernie Madoff, the swindler or, unfortunately, to Rachel Maddow, the left-wing television commentator, whom my parents watch every night before going to bed.

"She's not even Jewish," I tell them. "Although she does happen to be a lesbian." My parents are far more accepting than they used to be, but it doesn't hurt to point these things out from time to time.

"Really!" says my father. "How do you know all this?"

"How do you not know?" I say. "It was in the Sunday *Times*."

Max's early life, even more than that of most immigrants, was full of abrupt twists and turns, so much so that telling his story is, for me, irresistible.

"My parents married in the year 1863, when Czar Nicholas I freed the Russian peasants from serfdom and in the same year President Lincoln of the United States freed the colored people from slavery," Max began the typed manuscript he wrote at my Aunt Norma's request. The serfs were freed—sort of—in 1861, by Czar Alexander II, but never mind that. When I read this sentence of Max's, I realized that I am, after all, part of American history. Frankly, until then, I felt, basically, that I was a bystander.

As a child I noticed that my family celebrated certain holidays—Passover, Rosh Hashanah—and that my teachers made a big deal of others—Columbus Day, Washington's Birthday—and I concluded that these others must be Christian, which my classmates must be celebrating at home with appropriate festivities, as they did Christmas and Easter. Later, as a teenager with a growing political consciousness, it pleased me that so many leaders of the Left, Old and New, were Jewish like me and Abbie, and I concluded that as outsiders both in the countries from which we came and the one in which we currently found ourselves, we more than most could take a critical perspective.

Yet here is Max, "in a village far from civilization and surrounded by uncultured peasants," as he describes it, his father a religious boy with no experience outside the study house and afraid of everything, "a horse, a dog, a peasant." With good reason. A neighbor "put a match" to the straw roof of the family's home when Max was seven, incinerating everything they owned, although luckily the family themselves escaped. Yet Max could make the world-historical connections: his parents, the serfs, the slaves, the czar, the American president. And he's correct to do so, I think as I read his typescript. As the Buddhist said to the hot dog vendor, "Make me one with everything."

Max remembers *cheder*, Jewish school:

> I was four and a half years old. I wanted to play, run, and be outside on the street. I did not want to sit in a stuffy room, but it was forbidden a Jewish child to play. Only the peasant plays so he remains ignorant . . . On Saturday I was examined by my father. After the big Sabbath dinner he would rest. Then he would comb his beard and drink the tea. Then he would call me for an examination to see how much I had learned during the week . . . I knew I would be punished if I did not know the answers. My mother used to ask him why he hit me so hard—he would cripple me! I used to cry a lot. And run away to the forest, and pick berries on Saturday and eat them in spite, because it was against the Jewish law.

(My grandfather, too, remembers being punished for playing. "I do not remember when I was taken to school for the first time," he wrote in his little memoir, "but I do remember that the angel on high threw down a few cents to me from heaven to make sure that I learned well." Then:

> One time on a summer day, when they let us out of school one half hour before it became dark, I began to make a little wagon. I got two wheels that a non-Jewish kid gave me. I got a wooden box and a rounded stick for the axle. I worked at this creation with energy. A few friends helped me. Suddenly the Rebbe appeared. He saw what we were doing, and he

began to scream, "*Shkotsim!* Nonbelievers! Wagons are on your minds? Playthings?" And he broke the box, threw away the wheels and said, "Jewish children should not play with little wagons. Better you should go into the house and look in a book!"

My grandfather's apostasy, my father has told me, began on that very day; later, his rebellion was to smoke a cigarette in front of the synagogue on Yom Kippur.)

Although for Max's family, life in the village was difficult, lonely, and dangerous, it had its advantages. "Our home was completely surrounded by pine forests and blossoming gardens filled with the singing of birds," he writes. Visitors from the city came during the summer to breathe the fresh air—and to talk revolution. "I was so impressed by their idealism. They were sacrificing their young lives to free Russia of the Czar's despotism and for freedom for all nationalities that lived in Russia, in a heroic struggle for a better life for the peasants and workers."

In 1903 the government organized pogroms with the slogan "Kill the Jews and save Russia!"

"It made us more revolutionary," writes Max. "The agitators used to tell us the only protectors of the Jews was the working class." So Max decided to become a worker himself, and apprenticed himself to a bookbinder in the city of Gomel: this was when he was fourteen. It was 1905, the revolution, and there were strikes and riots all over Russia—and more pogroms. "Thousands were killed," he recounts, "but the young organized to defend themselves with arms, and they killed many hooligans." After the failure of the revolution, and the widespread pogroms, "many of the revolutionaries were disillusioned and left Russia for America," but Max stayed in Gomel to complete his apprenticeship. For a boy in the city earning eight rubles a month—"a good wage in those years for a beginner"—"life was very interesting": meetings, demonstrations, theater, opera.

Then, when he turned eighteen, he received his draft notice. He decided to emigrate and join his brother Ruben in New York—although not before being arrested in a sweep with twenty other young Jews, interrogated, and beaten. Luckily, he says, "my brother Mones had found out I was in jail, and as he had some pull with the big shots, they let me out." Making it back to his village, Max said goodbye to his family. "It was a very tragic departure. Never to see each other again. Going overseas to the United States of America. I left Russia full of hatred for the country in which I was born, never to come back."

So he thought.

In America, Max and Ruby worked in factories in New York and then in the Catskills for the summer peddling fruit and candy to the tourists, "walking from hotel to hotel, fifteen miles a day over the mountains." With their savings, Max says, "we both went on Main Street and bought derby hats with nice suits." (I can just see them. I so wish they'd had a photo taken.) Ever striving for something better, he and Ruby moved to Chicago, where they were joined by their sisters Ida and Hadeh. Max tried opening a store—Madoff Brothers—that quickly failed, worked as a paperhanger, ran a restaurant. "I tried various businesses with very little success," he sighs. "In the social atmosphere where I lived the viewpoint was that a socialist should be a worker and not a businessman, but I tried again and again to go into business."

Then came the First World War and the draft, that perpetual problem. Max quickly left Chicago for Montreal, where he encountered a large community of young Jewish men, there for the same reason as he. "I arrived in the big city of Montreal in the cold winter of November 1917," he recalls. "Many Russian Jews who lived in Canada were ready to go back to Russia. Meetings and lectures were held every day, and they all talked about the Russian revolution, the greatest in the history of mankind." The revolutionaries believed the capitalist war in Europe would drag on for untold years, and that eventually "the Canadian government would force all the young people to go into the military, regardless of what nationality."

So Max made his great decision: "With the inspiration of the Russian revolution, we, a small group of twelve people, decided not to wait out the war, but leave Canada and go to Japan. From Japan, we would go to Russia." If he had to fight, Max decided, he would fight for the revolution.

The first leg of their journey was a trip across Canada by train. "The Canadian scenery, the prairies and the Rocky Mountains, put us in a very good mood. We were full of hope for the future. We arrived in the beautiful city of Vancouver." Distractible and apparently still unable to read the "social atmosphere," Max says he then "proposed to some of the group to remain there and not leave the American continent. Maybe the war would end soon. They replied that I made a funny proposition: 'We are going to a socialist country. Down with capitalism!'"

Reinspired, he bought a ticket to Japan along with the rest of the group. The ship was packed, and when he asked the other passengers where they were going, "they answered that they were going to Russia to fight the counterrevolution. Everybody was happy, dancing and singing." The trip to Yokohama took two weeks.

When Max arrived in Japan he was full of wonder. It was as though he was on "a new planet . . . The people, their way of dressing, the walking with the wooden sandals and the noise they made while walking. The rickshaw transportation, a man pulling a little wagon and running very fast. The food they eat, rice and fish." The travelers met daily at the Yomasaka Hotel to "talk about the world situation. The intervention from the big powers against the Bolsheviks has begun. There was a civil war." Some decided at that point to return to the States; others to go to Mexico. Max wanted to wait it out in Japan and see what would happen next, so he and a few others rented a house. They were terribly lonely, and went to the port often to meet ships arriving from North America. "Every boat had people who were Russians and Jews with their wives and children, all going to Russia, to help build a socialist society."

One day, Max went to the port, and who should come climbing out of steerage but his brother Mones! "I asked him where he was going and what made him leave the U.S., as he wasn't drafted, and he wasn't going to Russia to fight in the civil war."

"I am anxious to go to my wife and children," Mones explained.

"It's ten thousand miles!" said Max. "Did our brother and sisters let you go?"

"No," said Mones, "but I went anyway."

Max hailed a rickshaw to take him and Mones to his house, but Mones refused to get in. "Are you crazy? A man will pull me?"

So they put Mones's luggage in the rickshaw and walked alongside, infuriating the driver, who probably thought they were cheapskates who simply didn't want to pay the fare. Then Mones refused to eat the food Max had prepared for him, because it wasn't kosher. A tone of exasperation creeps into Max's account when he says he then took Mones to Yokohama's Jewish Immigration House, which was full of Jews who had fled Russia by way of Manchuria and were on their way to the *goldeneh medinah,* the golden land, America. They were baffled to learn that Max and Mones were going the other way.

From here, in Max's narrative, things get confusing. Mones went to Harbin, China. Max went to Harbin, then to Mukden. They smuggled, they speculated, they got jobs as translators and clerks. Max typed invoices in Russian for a Jewish furrier in Mukden for eighteen months; then the Bolsheviks won the war in Russia, the fur trade from Siberia dried up, the furrier went out of business, and Max had to decide: "to go to Canada or go to Russia to see my parents and my family." By then, he writes, "I was sure I was not going to stay in Russia. I had heard so much about the hard life in a Communist dictatorship, with no freedom, but as I still had a desire to see my people, I decided to go." Who wouldn't? Max seems to imply. He got on a train, but because parts of the route went through territory that was occupied by White Russians, it took him only as far as the Mongolian border. So he and a few other passengers decided to cross Mongolia on horseback.

Horseback! But why shouldn't a Jew ride a horse? Ever on the lookout for a little business, Max put up the money for the horses, and when they got to Russia, he planned to sell them at a profit.

At this point in the story, Mones turns up again and begs Max to take him along. "I told him it would be a very hard trip and that he wouldn't have any kosher food," Max writes. "He said that he would live on sardines."

On the first day, Mones ate his sardines for lunch, became thirsty, and in desperation, drank from a puddle. Immediately, he came down with dysentery.

On the second day, Mones told Max he was dying, and begged him to find a house for him to die in, so he wouldn't expire in an open field.

On the third day, Max somehow located a Russian family, who took Mones into their home. Only one thing, Max warned the family before he left Mones with them for the night: "Do not give him any milk."

Max went to buy rice, which he had been told back in Harbin was the best cure for diarrhea. The next morning he returned with a twenty-pound bag, only to find Mones "lying on the sofa, very sick, drinking milk."

"You're poisoning yourself! You're committing suicide!" Max shouted, grabbing the milk from Mones's hand. "I started to cook rice," he writes. "I gave him the juice of the rice to drink the whole day long. The next day he began to feel better, and we started on our trip again.

"We did not know when we left Harbin how dangerous it was to travel in Mongolia," says Max. They had since learned that the country was full of bandits, who would kill anyone they met—"especially Jews," he explains. Since the bandits probably didn't have many opportunities to kill Jews in the Asiatic wilderness, Max's group would have made an attractive target. Max bought a revolver, "but it did not shoot at all times. Sometimes it did, and then again it didn't."

Max, Mones, and their group arrived in Urga (now Ulan Bator), the Mongolian capital, just in time for the High Holidays. As on all their other stops, they met a group of Jews who were fleeing Russia. "They saved some of their wealth in gold and they had plans to go to Palestine through China," Max says of this contingent, whose understanding of geography seems to have been somewhat desperate. Mones volunteered to lead them in Rosh Hashanah services. "He was the only Jew among them who knew how to sing and pray and ask God Almighty for a happy New Year. The women thanked him very much. When they heard him praying they cried and he, after all the sicknesses he had, did his best on those Rosh Hashanah days."

The holiday over, Max tried and failed to sell the horses. His investment was lost. The group traveled to the border in a wagon, and there they parted ways, taking trains to various parts of Russia. Max ended up in the Siberian city of Irkutsk, which was freezing and dangerous, full of killers and thieves on horses or sleds, who would "throw a rope over your head like the American cowboys lasso their cattle, take off your clothes and leave you naked in the zero weather." Typhus and other diseases were epidemic; "posters in the streets appealed to the citizens to go to the bathhouse and change the underwear often." Robbers went free in this upside-down world, and innocents were jailed, says Max. The people were hungry and sick; their leaders were hypocritical and corrupt.

It was only when Max arrived in Irkutsk, Russia, his goal of so many years, that he finally ran out of energy and hope. "For twelve days I was in the city, inspecting many institutions and trials in the courts and getting all the information I could from many people," he says. "I came to the conclusion that they were afraid of the truth . . . I realized there was no hope for mankind of a better society of justice and truth. I did not see very much justice and not much truth."

Max ran into a man he knew from Yokohama: small world. There, Max says, the man had been "an enemy of the Bolsheviks, very conservative"—but in Irkutsk, he was the chairman of the Communist Party. He offered to get Max a ticket to Moscow, from which Max would be able to travel to his native village and his parents.

It was his last chance to see his family, but if he went, he understood, he'd never be allowed to leave. "I decided not to go any further," writes Max sadly. "All my plans to see my people and make the dangerous trip in the cold zero weather for thousands of miles from Siberia were over."

Is this why this is such a great story? Because after all his trials, Max never reaches his destination, but courageously turns around, rendering his entire journey absurd, the Odyssey reconceived by Samuel Beckett and Mickey Katz?

My mother says Max has no place in this family history, because he was not a blood relation—but first of all, as Madoff, he must have been, however distant and confused; and second of all, that is so atavistic. Are we ancient Hebrews or Israeli rabbis who must trace our descent matrilineally because it's the only way of making sure we don't have a cuckoo in our midst? We gay people have a saying: "Love makes a family"—and I love Max.

Mickey Katz, by the way, was a Jewish vaudevillian writer

of humorous songs including "Duvid Crockett" and "Borscht Riders in the Sky." He would have howled at the idea of Max leading his lost tribe on horseback through the Mongolian steppes.

Returning to Irkutsk on the train, Max's perceptions had changed. He observed "men and women carrying large sacks of flour on their backs . . . moving like white silhouettes . . . mountains of snow and ice surrounding us . . . everything is white." The country was populated by bent and struggling ghosts. Life unraveled backwards. Max made his way back to Harbin, back to Yokohama, back over the Pacific Ocean to Vancouver, back across Canada to Windsor, Ontario, where he was met by his family. "I was again a new immigrant," writes Max. "Fifteen years after my first landing in New York, I had to start life all over again. I began re-examining my past with new hopes"—of course—"for a better future."

He discovered that Sorke, whom he'd dated briefly before his journey, was not yet married. "We met again and renewed our young love at an older age after we had more experience in life," Max concludes. "We got married in June 1923 and had a son the next year, then a daughter. We have been married more than half a century and we have had much happiness."

# my bat mitzvah

**My Dress.** Jean and Abe Lipstadt were friends of my parents from temple, a childless couple who wanted us to consider them our honorary aunt and uncle. At their request, my parents gave us *special permission* to call them by their first names rather than Mr. and Mrs., the honorifics we were required to use with other adults. Jean seemed to want me, especially, to feel close to her, but I never did, despite her kindness and attention to me. At one time she had played the violin, and she encouraged me in my lessons, lending me her instrument so I wouldn't have to use the crummy school one and giving me a recording of the Sibelius concerto for my birthday. Then, she offered to make my bat mitzvah dress. She invited me to her house for lunch, just the two of us, tuna sandwiches, and afterward took me to the fabric store to pick out a pattern and material.

"Do you like this one?"

"It's nice."

"What about this?"

"That's okay too."

The pattern books were huge, and I knew the perfect dress must be in them somewhere but also that Jean would never find it. She finally chose for me: a simple A-line shift with a round neck and a small bow at the waist, to be made out of a deep-red brocade.

"You'll look beautiful in this, dear," Jean assured me. "And your mother will love it. It's classic."

"Great, thank you," I said. I had no alternative to suggest, but classic wasn't what I'd had in mind. I wanted total transformation—Cinderella finally facing down all those wicked stepsisters at school with their Villager blouses and twinsets from Bernie's, where I often slinked around, avoiding the saleswomen and never buying anything. It was unthinkable, on my allowance.

At least I'd get to wear stockings and heels instead of my usual kneesocks and oxfords. My mother had already bought me the garter belt I would need (only later, in high school, did I adopt the Thoreauvian principle of passing up any outfit that required special underwear). And the week before I had started junior high school my parents' friend Shirley Jacobs, a tall, intimidating woman with bleached blonde hair and a shelf of a bosom, had paid my mother a visit. Shirley, whose daughter Rhonda was a year older than me, taught my Hebrew school class, and when Shirley left, my mother took me shopping for a bra. It may just have been coincidence, but I've always connected the two occurrences and assumed that Shirley had come to tell my mother that if I didn't stop wearing undershirts I'd be endlessly taunted in gym class. I knew this as well as Shirley did—over the summer, when the granddaughters of our neighbors, the Roths, had come to visit them in the Berkshires, they'd spied the soft, dark hairs under my arms, which had given them hours of amusement—but I'd resigned myself. I couldn't figure out how to explain my life to my mother. With her immigrant parents and Depression upbringing, she seemed innocent of the requirements of American adolescence and the ways of our high schools. I felt this even though I knew she'd been to high school herself, James Monroe in the Bronx, where according to her stories she'd had a clique of friends, gone to dances, spoken

French, and been a cheerleader, which at the time involved wearing a long skirt and saddle shoes. But I was her good girl, with two long braids that she combed for me every morning and day-of-the-week panties.

I wanted the bra, but I didn't quite get its purpose. Okay, I understood, you needed it for the locker room. But it was uncomfortable, especially the band around my chest, of which I could never shake my awareness, so I felt like I was perpetually wearing one of those hideous midriff blouses with puffy sleeves. And then I went to a slumber party, and in front of the other girls, including Rhonda, took off my shirt and put on my pajama top, and they shrieked, "What are you doing? Look at her, she's wearing her bra to bed!" According to them this would stunt my growth; it probably explained why I didn't need the bra in the first place. Then they had a long discussion of the facts of life, which I'd known perfectly well since I was about five, since my mother was so often pregnant, but at that moment I was appalled.

I wore my bat mitzvah dress only once. Something about it wasn't right. It was like a girlfriend I had much later in life: none of my friends ever warmed up to her. They never said anything directly, but I could tell she made them uncomfortable. What I couldn't tell was why—what exactly was wrong with her. With the girlfriend, I eventually figured it out: she was crazy, and everyone but me had picked up on her crazy vibes right from the start. But I still couldn't tell you exactly what the problem was with the dress.

My Relatives.   Most of the people who showed up for my bat mitzvah I'd never seen before in my life and would never see again, like Great-Aunt Sylvia Fish from Sioux City, Iowa, an enormous woman who brought as her gift several shoeboxes-full of her famous *taiglach*, little marbles of dough coated with honey, waxed paper separating the sticky layers. *"A meichel,"* said my grandmother, her older sister. "Very tasty." They were just the sort of thing she loved, sweet, crunchy, and you could sample a couple on the fly, without having to sit still for an actual meal.

"How did Sylvia end up in Sioux City, anyway?" I e-mail my father. Most of the Madorskys had wandered no farther west than Detroit.

He responds, all in caps. No one's told him that in e-mail this is impolite, like shouting—actually, this seems appropriate, since our real conversations are shouted. "ALL I KNOW IS THAT SYLVIA MARRIED LOU FISH WHO WAS WIDOWED WITH TWO YOUNG CHILDREN. LOU'S FATHER HAD SETTLED IN SIOUX CITY IN THE LATE 19TH CENTURY AND TRADED WITH THE FARMERS AND THEN STARTED A WHOLESALE GASOLINE AND TRUCK TIRE BUSINESS. THEY WERE THE U.S. RUBBER DISTRIBUTORS IN IOWA FOR YEARS."

I have so much respect for these immigrant entrepreneurs: wholesale truck tires, what would they think of next?

My grandmother was less pleased with some of the other siblings who showed up, especially her brother Louie. "A dummy," she said. "*Farshtupte kopf.*" Stuffed head, but not with brains. We kids were delighted by the way their childhood tensions persisted even into old age. I don't know what he'd done to offend her, but the epithet stuck, and even now, if you say to someone in my family, "Louie," the other person responds, "Ha! *farshtupte kopf.*" Yet he was undistinguishable from the rest: short, chubby, switching all the time from garbled English to incomprehensible Yiddish.

The sensation of the weekend was Uncle Yossel. He was ninety years old! Every time he encountered a child, he would slip him or her a five-dollar bill. My father told us to give Yossel his money back, but Yossel waved it away.

"I loved that guy," my father tells me now. In Russia, Yossel had been a revolutionary. "In 1905 he was making bombs."

"*He* was?" I ask. I know this story already, or at least I think I do. "I thought that was Grandpa's sister Gittel. Out back, in the barn."

"Nah, that was Yossel," says my father. "One of the bombs went off before it should have, and he knew the authorities would be coming for him, so he skedaddled." In Russia, he adds, Yossel had had a wife and two children.

"So what happened to them?" asks my mother.

"What? What? Who knows?" my father shrugs, uncharacteristically, since for him, this is the worst thing, perhaps even more terrible than bombs. For him, taking care of your family is the very purpose and definition of manhood, but with Yossel, he refrained from judgment. Pogroms, revolution, conscription, prison—how can we in our comfortable lives condemn?

And, after all, maybe we don't have to, because my Aunt Norma shows me a photograph of Yossel, Gittel, and my grandfather—all together, in Russia. So maybe the story of Yossel's first family in the old country was a myth, since he was already with Gittel there. In America, Yossel married her and started a plumbing supply company: Joe Simon and Sons. Then, his sons edged him out of the business.

"Yossel, that's terrible, why didn't you do something?" my father had asked him.

"I should fight with family?" said Yossel.

"A gentle soul," my father concludes.

"*A gute neshameh*," explains my mother.

The day after the bat mitzvah, the great-aunts and -uncles decided to go into Manhattan, to walk around the Lower East Side, where they had once lived. Tentatively, they invited me to come with them—why would a thirteen-year-old be interested in their tenements and stories? And they were right, I wasn't, and I was shy of spending a whole day with them, old people whom I barely knew. But I accepted immediately. I couldn't turn down a chance to go to New York, whose skyline you could see from the windows of my Hebrew school classroom, like Oz in the distance.

It had been such a long time since they'd been to the Lower East Side that they kept getting lost in the narrow streets, but every once in a while, one of them would point to a building and say, "That's it. I'm sure. See the fire escape? We used to sleep out there, in the hot weather." For lunch they took me to Ratner's Dairy Restaurant on Delancey Street, where the surly waiters put out a whole basket of fresh rolls on the table and brought more when those were gone.

"Take a few in your purse, sweetheart," the aunts and uncles instructed me. "To eat later on the bus."

My Presents.    Mostly I got checks, which went into an account to be saved for a trip to Israel when I was older. But there were also a lot of boxes to open. A distant cousin sat in the room with me while I ripped them apart. A fine gold chain with a small pearl. Two pocketbooks, one brown marshmallow leather, and the other quilted black vinyl, fake-Chanel, which my mother still uses. Then I opened a final package and was struck speechless: a genuine Villager blouse—long sleeves, round collar, in a pattern of tiny pink and red roses, and a cranberry-red A-line skirt to go with it.

"It must be from Bernie's," I breathed.

"Is that an exclusive store?" asked the cousin.

I have no idea what she meant—maybe something like those boutiques that appear in old movies when the husband or a girlfriend of the mousy female protagonist wants to buy her the right kinds of clothes. No other shoppers are in these boutiques, and the clothes are not hanging on racks but instead chosen for and displayed to the shopper by the salesgirl. The shopper disappears into the back and reappears transformed.

I don't remember who picked that gift for me—some truly kind and insightful person whom I hope I thanked—and the skirt and blouse were my favorite outfit for years. They fit perfectly, the sleeves of the blouse long enough and the skirt short enough, so I didn't have to roll it up at the waist after I left the house in the morning, evading my mother's critical eye.

My Speech.   In some temples the rabbi tells you what to talk about, but I chose my own topic for my bat mitzvah speech, and no one waved me away from it, although it was predictable that I'd become embarrassed about it later. I discussed the first chapter of Genesis, because I believed I'd discovered something momentous about it: namely, that rather than conflicting with evolutionary theory, the Creation story took it into account. I didn't get into the logical problem of the separation of day from night before the placement of the sun and the moon, which I hadn't noticed; nor into the mysterious circumstance of the waters below and the waters above, held back from drowning the universe by the inverted bowl of the firmament; nor into the issue that after God rests on the seventh day, He starts in creating the world all over again in Genesis two. But just look at the primeval Days: after the geologic upheavals that result in the oceans and continents, you get the sea creatures, then the animals that crawl on land, then the beasts of the field, and finally human beings. The evolutionary progression. Religion and science need not conflict. Problem solved.

Odd, that this reconciliation of scripture and reason was so important to me. I was an earnest child, the type whom the rabbis characterized as "wise"; the type who, they said, asks at the seder, "What are the testimonies, the statutes and the laws which the Lord, our God, has commanded?" Although the rabbis' categorization of children into only four types—wise, wicked, indifferent, and clueless—shows, says my mother, that they didn't know so much. Nevertheless, every Friday evening in our home she draped a lace scarf over her head and lit candles. Quietly, she would say, "We welcome in the Sabbath Queen," and circle her arms three times over the flames, as though to pull them toward her, and sing the ancient prayer, all strange intervals and melismas. My father gruffly blessed the wine, we ate a chicken, and then we went to temple for the Shabbat service. Sometimes we returned there on Saturday morning. How the congregation loved our large family, my mother always with a baby in her arms. It was proof that despite Man's best effort, God's people would not disappear from the earth; a promise, like the dove and the rainbow, that the generations would flourish.

Yet my parents are, and always have been, unbelievers, convinced that organized religion is a haven of superstition and fanaticism—although that doesn't at all disrupt their Jewish identity or their observance of rituals and holidays. I am, too, and so, I suspect, are the rest of my siblings. We just don't have the gene of faith—because some scientists now say it's inherent in the brain, one of Homo sapiens's built-in capacities, like language. If so, we're lacking it, like a family of dyslexics. We try, making out scripture to be a guide to rational living—Genesis as pointing toward modern science; monotheism as the antidote to superstition; circumcision and dietary laws as healthy innovations. Weren't the ancients wise! But the faithful follow the laws because God said so and for no other reason; they go berserk if they use the wrong fork. The laws aren't wise at all, they're insane—and that's the whole point, the more insane the better, to prove one's faith.

My family weren't Jews because of God, we were Jews because we were Jews. "Never, ever deny that," my parents taught us. Because even here in America, they whispered, "if you forget, a *goy* will remind you." The punishment for assimilation is

Holocaust. So, on Yom Kippur we beat our breasts, on Hanukkah we exchanged gifts, on Purim we dressed in costumes, and on Passover we brought matzo sandwiches to school for a week, causing hilarity in the cafeteria. We celebrated even the more obscure holidays, like Tu B'Shvat, the holiday of the plant kingdom, when we donated our nickels and dimes to sow trees in Israel, and some day we would go up there to see our forests.

In the venerable old joke, a Jew washes up on a desert island. His rescuers are astonished to find that he has built three synagogues. The Jew gives them a tour: "This one I go to every week, and this one I go to on the high holidays. And that one? *Feh!* That one I would never go to!" That's my father. His religion is arguing with the rabbi and debunking his sermons. "The earth stood still? The waters parted? *Please.*" A scientist, he comes back from services fuming: "The guy's an imbecile." Yet throughout our childhood and beyond, he kept going. He was the president of the temple. He raised money for the United Jewish Appeal. He likes the story of Isaac, who wrestled all night with God. Now *there's* an ancestor with a real *yiddishe kopf*—the true Jewish mentality.

As for me, I learned the entire shabbat service by heart for my bat mitzvah—including the Torah blessings, although I was not allowed to say them, even at my temple, where the rabbi had three daughters, which is why we ignored many of the restrictions on women and celebrated bat mitzvahs, for example. I felt guilty about my unbelief. I wanted to belong, to find comfort in the holy words and modal harmonies, but I couldn't. They meant nothing to me.

### The Bat Mitzvah Crown. 
My mother's father made me a crown. For a living, he had sewn and then peddled ties, and now, at the senior center, they had him making jewelry. He wrapped plastic gimp around metal cuffs to make bracelets,

which he gave to my sisters and me. We would wear them for an afternoon, then misplace and forget about them. To make the crown, my grandfather had riveted colored rhinestones onto shiny white acetate, embroidered it with gold, silver, and crimson thread, and tacked it onto a cardboard template.

At the reception, as I was presiding over my table, flanked by the kids from my Hebrew school class, he presented me with the crown. My mother came with him and stood behind me. She put her hands on my shoulders and bent down to kiss my cheek. I knew what she wanted. I could feel her, silently begging me to wear the crown. To please him. To please her. She knew as well as I that it was a strange and ugly thing, but she pretended to me and to her father that it was a unique and beautiful gift, just as she pretended to me and to him that he was a sane and loving grandfather. After all, that was the way things should have been. She was counting on me to come through for her and to act as though I were proud and happy to wear the bat mitzvah crown. She was trying so hard to believe it was beautiful, and that I was proud. She needed my help, and I never could refuse her.

This was exactly the kind of thing that drove me crazy about her. She rejected the obvious. And then she said I was the one who was living in a dream. I dawdled. I showed up late. I lost my glasses. In school I had my head in a book, so I didn't hear the teacher when she went on to the next activity. Arithmetic. I didn't know the answer. For years, I placed things before my mother that she refused to see. I flaunted cigarettes, reefer, birth control pills. Or conversely I told her nothing and left it to her to ask, knowing she never would, although of course it pained her not to.

She smiled down at me and placed the crown on my head. She didn't save me from humiliation, nor did I expect her to. I was now an adult, and she thrust me forward to do my duty.

Throughout the meal, eaten with heavy silverware, I could feel the weight of the bat mitzvah crown upon my head.

Then I must have taken it off, stood up from the table, and rushed to join the dancing and playing, leaving it to be cleared away with the dirty dishes.

# the jewish policeman

In my early twenties I dated a lovely Jewish guy—yes, a guy. I wanted to be a lesbian, but none of the women I had crushes on would even look at me, which is not surprising since I did nothing to let them know my feelings. On the contrary I did my best to conceal them, not out of shame about the nature of my desires but rather out of awe: I didn't dare address a word to those marvelous creatures. In the meantime, here was this Jeffrey, inviting me to restaurants and concerts, picking up the checks, and finding my identity as a "strong woman," as he called it, a turn-on, although in my ambivalence I would secretly rage, when he expressed his admiration: Do you think I developed myself—marched in the streets, paid the rent, patched my bicycle tires—for *you*?

But to continue: in my early twenties, I dated a lovely Jewish guy whose father was a cop in New York City. My parents would have been so pleased about it—guy, Jew—but they were never to hear of this relationship. I didn't share with them the details of my personal life, if only because it was too confusing. I'd already told them I was gay.

"You're kidding," I said to Jeff. "So's my uncle." My Uncle Marty the cop, the husband of my mother's sister Pearl, had a square, rough face, black hair brushed back from a high forehead, and a certain kind of crooked, clenched-toothed grin that I associate with people from the Bronx: Pearl had it too, and sometimes even my mother, and Roberta, my love. He smoked cigars. Even today, on the street, I pass some old man trailing smoke, and a memory wafts into my mind: Marty. You could tell when he'd been in our house.

"Maybe they know each other," said Jeffrey, grasping at any straw of connection he could find to reinforce our crumbling relationship. I'd told him, too, that I was gay. Mostly. "My dad belongs to the *Shomrim* Society," he said. "For Jewish cops. There aren't that many of them."

Marty had in fact been an active brother in the society, but he was long retired at that point, and when Jeffrey asked, his dad had never heard of him.

According to my father, Marty was just about the only honest cop in New York City, he and the other *Shomrim*. Marty wouldn't take even a Thanksgiving turkey, my father told me proudly.

Usually the brothers-in-law in my family got along well, peacefully retreating to the bedroom to watch football when we gathered for holidays, but they had a memorable blow-up at the Passover seder in 1969, over the New York mayoral election between the working-class Democrat Mario Procaccino and the "limousine liberal" Republican John Lindsay. Marty and my Uncle Walter favored Procaccino, who was for law-and-order and for government to stop tying the hands of the police; my father favored Lindsay, who was not like a Republican at all, opposing the war in Vietnam and supporting civil rights for black people. For months after the fight the little kids in the family took up the chant, "Ma-rio Pro-caccino! Ma-rio Pro-caccino!"

It was the same year that Betty and Bobby, Marty and Pearl's twins, became hippies and moved to Vermont, reappearing in the city every once in a while to do things like sell Christmas trees on the street corner to make money for their commune.

Until then, they'd never been much interested in me, nor I in them, Betty especially having been an intimidating high school hoodlum who ratted up her blonde hair, wore heavy black cat's-eye makeup, and plausibly claimed to be several years older than her twin. She hated it when he turned up, undermining her performance. But now that they were living on the commune, something about my long braids and my Joan Baez album appealed to them, my shyness perhaps looking like inner peace. Betty gave me a gift of *The Freewheelin' Bob Dylan*—"He sings so fucky," she said—and spent an afternoon helping me to make a fringed hippie poncho out of an old plaid blanket.

The class antagonism that underlay the Mario Procaccino brawl went over my head. In my mother's family, she was the one who got away. With Pearl and Toby, her two older sisters, working and helping to support the family, my mother was able to go to college, marry, move to New Jersey—while they got only as far from the Bronx as Queens. Our families visited back and forth, and spent holidays together, Hanukkah and Passover, although no one ever arrived to our joint seders on time because of the traffic. "Half the Jews in New York going to visit the other half," says my mother. Some years we were so late in getting started that one of us ended up knocking over the glass of red wine onto the white tablecloth before Cousin Phyllis, Toby's daughter, could do it. With great affection, my mother always set the table with the stain in front of her place. None of us could understand my mother's closeness to Phyllis—although she was our cousin, she was closer to our parents' generation than ours; my mother had been her babysitter. Phyllis had a terrible reputation among us for flakiness and lack of tact: she cast horoscopes, read cards, and thinking she was complimenting me said of my high school graduation photo, "Why, the ugly duckling has turned into a swan!" These days she's the successful author of books on astrology, numerology, and tarot, and how to use these disciplines to spice up your love life and pick the right baby name. She sends them to my parents as gifts.

"Who reads this garbage?" my father asks me, then muses, "Someone must. Amy, why don't you write books like this?" Phyllis outsells me by a large margin.

Pearl died in her early seventies of lung cancer, which infuriated my mother even as she mourned her, since my mother has never let a cigarette touch her lips and had often nagged Pearl to quit. Walter had died by then, too, and with their spouses gone and loneliness setting in, Marty and Toby married, an unexpected coda of comfort and affection in their old age.

I should end the story here, with the couple my aunt and uncle twice over. The calm shatters, though, when the coda becomes an interlude, because after Marty died, Bobby and Toby became locked into a stupid dispute over Marty's will. Bobby was stubborn; mediation was impossible. He broke with Betty as well, convinced that she, too, owed him part of her legacy. I suppose he'd become quite paranoid, although at the time no one understood his symptoms, they were just mad at him for being such a *schmuck*.

Actually even before all that no one in my family had been speaking much to Bobby; my father had cut him off back when he had left the commune and refused to support his daughter, Star Scarlett. In Bobby's defense, he couldn't have had much money to send. He'd moved back to the Bronx, and one afternoon he invited me to see his apartment. His only furniture was a couple of stereo speakers the size of refrigerators. He was excited about his plan to paint the place six colors, and I helped him with the kitchen. When we knocked off for the day, he put a record on the turntable, and we sat on the floor in front of the giant speakers. He offered me a joint. It was the first time I'd been in that situation, and unsure of what to do with it, and what it would do to me—not to mention well-aware that even if he was a hippie he was also an older family member, with a direct line to my parents—I touched it to my lips and passed it back to him. "Good girl," said Bobby. "Don't bogart it."

Betty eventually left the commune too, and moved to San Francisco with her baby, Jossamber Thistle—the names the hippies gave their children fascinated us, and my mother made silly jokes about the problems that would arise if the little girl grew up to have a lisp: Jothamber Thithle Thtevens. Of course, that was assuming Joss took her father's name, Stevens, which my mother of course did assume. Jossamber, we were informed, is a flavor of incense. This, too, was interesting: so incense came in flavors, not scents.

When Jossamber was born, my mother had told us, "Your Cousin Betty got married and had a baby!" Then, a few years later, she had more news: "Betty got married!"

"But wasn't she already married?"

"Well," she admitted, "No."

"Jesus, Ma! So this time she's really married?"

It's unclear. In San Francisco, Betty had a son, Moss—later he changed his name to Scott—with a fellow who was a conductor on the cable cars. Then, in her mid-thirties, she was diagnosed with breast cancer. At first she wanted to treat it naturally—herbs, massage, a sojourn at a clinic in Mexico. We received reports on her health from Phyllis, who had always been close to the twins. "Betty would love to hear from you," she urged me. "She thinks you're very put-together."

" 'Together.' "

"What?" said Phyllis.

"It's just 'together,' " I said. "Not 'put.' "

Phyllis was right about getting in touch, I knew that. But writing Betty a letter was hard. I didn't know what to say about her illness, and I couldn't think of anything that might interest her—or anyone—about my life: day job, contentious feminist meetings, sexual hopelessness, Jeffrey. "Dear Betty, I still listen to *Freewheelin'*. I'm dating a guy whose father is a Jewish police-man in New York, like yours was. Get well soon." It wouldn't do. Anyway, I was going to break up with him any minute. So I put it off. For years.

And Betty did get well, for a long time, but then her cancer recurred, and at the end, my father phoned Bobby and said, "Call your sister. Please," but Bobby refused to yield. Betty was cared for and mourned by her daughter and son, and other friends and relatives—Phyllis, my parents—but not by her twin.

Not long ago, Phyllis kindly friended me on Facebook, where she'd posted a bunch of old photos, and I realized something: Betty was the most physically beautiful person my family, either side, ever produced, with wavy red-blonde hair, creamy skin, a joyful, open smile. Bobby was dark, a good-looking guy, sure, but nothing to touch her. Before her cancer. It hurts to see her. I wish so many things. That I had known her well enough to have been a comfort. That I had at least given her a hug.

Several years after Betty's death, unreconciled and alone, Bobby shot himself. Such a violent and terrible act, he must have had serious problems all along.

# jazzin' with the greats

I keep a photo on my bookshelf of me and my father, dancing at my brother Josh's wedding, October 1995, Hartford, Connecticut. My father's bow tie is slightly askew, and he's half-smiling, his right arm around my shoulder and my left hand in his, in the classic ballroom clasp. He's wearing a rented tuxedo with a pink shirt and a boutonniere.

He owns a tuxedo that he inherited from his brother-in-law, my Uncle Walter, but Joshua didn't want him to wear it. They argued about it. "It's double-breasted, Dad. It doesn't match anyone else's. It doesn't even fit you right."

"It fits me fine," he said. "I loved that guy."

When my mother's sister Toby met Walter, my father tells me, Walter was driving a truck for a slaughterhouse. The job was disgusting, and he hated it, coming home stinking of animal fat, his clothes ruined. My grandmother suggested, "Why don't you find something else?"

So for a long time, he drove a cab. Then, when Charley, his daughter Phyllis's husband, got out of the military, the two of them bought a truck and made deliveries all over New York City, which Walter knew, from the cab, like the back of his hand.

Business wasn't bad. Toby and Walter lived in a high rise in Flushing Meadows, with Charley and Phyllis down the hall—the name of their neighborhood a cause for great glee among my brothers and sisters and me, whenever we drove out to visit. We could tell we were getting close when we passed Shea Stadium and the 1964 World's Fair grounds, the Unisphere now surrounded by brush and looking sad and rusted. Seeing it, though, would remind me of its heyday, when my father and Uncle Walter had taken us to the fair, where we waited on endless lines to see Disney's animatronic Lincoln deliver the Gettysburg Address, and General Electric's dioramas of kitchens past and future. In the kitchen of the past was a small ice box with a big round motor on the top, and we kids began yelling, "That's our refrigerator!" because it was just like the one we had at the lake, the cottage having come supplied with Mrs. Roth's antique appliances. Embarrassed lest the crowd think we couldn't afford something more up to date, my father explained loudly, "In our *summer* house, our *summer* house." The talk of the fair was a fabulous confection called a Belgian waffle, and I was curious about it but never got to experience one. The wait to buy them was so long and the waffles so overpriced that we went back to the apartment instead, where Toby served us supermarket cookies.

I loved Toby and Walter's apartment. Toby, her hair dyed bright red, would set out cut-glass dishes of cigarettes and candy in the living room, which was decorated with a wallpaper mural of an oasis, weeping willows and palms surrounding a tranquil pool. It was so beautiful. I would tug my mother's skirt: "Why can't *we* have that?"

Walter's favorite avocation was shopping for clothes. The word "dapper" was made for him; he was the only man I knew with a mustache, and even if I never saw him in a straw boater— and I may have—that's how I picture him. When he and Toby came to visit us in Rutherford, my father would take him downtown to Zimmerman's, a menswear store run by a friend of his from the temple. At one Zimmerman's sale, my father bought a beautiful camel's hair coat, and Walter agonized over a white leather jacket, trying it on, turning this way and that in the three-way mirror. It would have been perfect for watching football on Hanukkah, when my father, my brothers, and my uncles sequestered themselves in my parents' bedroom, one game playing on the TV with the sound turned off and a second one on the radio. Walter would wear a special outfit in honor of his favorite player, Joe Namath of the New York Jets: white patent-leather loafers and a matching belt—what's called the Full Cleveland. But finally he put the jacket back on the rack. White is totally impractical; he could just see it after a day in the truck.

Eventually, Walter got a job in the mail room of one of his delivery customers, a position he adored, because he could wear a suit—a different one every day—to work. He sold the truck and began driving around in a pink Cadillac. Sadly, though, he didn't get to enjoy his white-collar job or his slow-boat of a car for very long. The stomach pains that had tormented him for a year were diagnosed as pancreatic cancer. When my father visited him in the hospital, Walter gestured to him. He had something final to say, a deathbed insight. My father leaned in close, and Walter whispered hoarsely in his ear, "I shoulda bought the jacket."

My father inherited Walter's wardrobe, and the Cadillac was sold to my parents' friend Jerry Bean, who got into some sort of weird dispute with Walter's brother about the tires and came home one day to find them all missing, the car up on blocks.

So that's why my father wanted to wear his outmoded tuxedo to Josh's wedding—all that history woven into its shiny lapels. A few weeks before the wedding, I had ridden my bicycle from Boston to New York in an AIDS fundraiser, a feat for which I'd trained for months. I'd never done anything remotely like it before, so I was feeling very proud and fit, in great shape to wear a clingy dress and to show myself off to the new in-laws by dancing with my father. At previous weddings I'd danced with no one, not with my girlfriend of the moment, who'd been

politely invited, but who, I understood, was to make herself
scarce once we got to the celebration, and not with my father.
With his discomfort at my lesbianism, dancing, though traditional and sweet, had been just too awkward. But he was letting
go of that, and I was letting go in turn of my own resentments
and disappointments. My father and I rose from our chairs,
and the photographer asked us to pose. My father put his arm
around my back and took my hand in his.

My parents used to love to dance and did it at every opportu-
nity: in the living room when a song they knew came on the
radio or TV, at weddings, bar mitzvahs, and birthday parties,
my father suavely leading my mother around the floor. We
kids would cringe and refuse to be drawn into their arms when
they invited us to join them. I was acutely conscious, dancing
at Josh's wedding, of how much less graceful I was than my
mother, no good at following at all—one more thing she can
do that I'll never master, like the way she can fold a fitted sheet
into a perfect rectangle.

Priscilla once asked my father, teasing, "But who do you love
the best?" and he didn't pretend neutrality as usual. He said,
"Amy was our first, and she is special." Then, at the family
Hanukah party, hosted by Priscilla, he didn't even notice me
standing in the kitchen, and I teased him: "Hey, Daddy, you
hugged everybody but me!" and he said, "Aah, you're the oldest,
you can live without a hug."

Josh's wedding took place back when my parents could still
dance, before my father's spine surgery and my mother's heart
attacks. Recently she's complained of feeling bored at the lake.
She doesn't have the strength for her usual walks and errands,
and we're all concerned that this will lead to a bout of depression.

She'd experienced them before, during the summer after her
first hospitalizations for heart disease. She became confused

during her weekly trip to the Great Barrington Price Chopper—which only confirmed my belief that that store is bad news. For years its logo pictured an axe splitting a coin, on which was the silhouette of a woman's head. Some horrified corporate marketer must finally have noticed, because the coin is now just a bland circle with some patriotic stars decorating the circumference. My mother forgot which aisle she was in and what she'd come for, and my sister-in-law had to lead her back to the car and drive her home. She lay on the couch, my busy mother, anxiously counting the knotholes in the pine paneling, which stared back at her like eyes. She called me, trembling. "I can't focus on anything. I can't read a book. I can barely finish the op-ed page of the *New York Times*."

"The op-ed page of the *Times*?" I said. "Ma, you can't be that bad off."

But she thought she was losing her mind.

So this time I drive out to the lake and take her to the symphony rehearsal at Tanglewood. As the players wander onto the stage in their shorts and baseball caps, she says, resolutely, "I'm going to enjoy this." Frankly she looks miserable, and I wonder if we should just turn around and go home.

"Look, Ma," I point out, paging through the program. "They have a jazz series. Maybe you should get tickets to that."

My mother doesn't need me to tell her what to do. "It's not *our* jazz," she says. It must be some kind of fusion or bebop; she and my father like the classics of the thirties and forties. With her silver hair and her skinny, wrinkled arms, she often wears a tee-shirt she received for making a contribution to public radio: "WBGO Newark: Jazzin' with the Greats." It has cartoon drawings on it of Louie and Ella. "Next week in Great Barrington we're going to hear the Count Basie Orchestra. Of course," she adds, in case I don't know what she's talking about, "Count Basie himself is dead."

"Yes," I say.

She'd seen them all: the Duke, the Count, Lady Day, with her gardenia in her hair. My mother says "God Bless the Child" contains her favorite song lyric: "God bless the child who's got his own." That's how you make your way in this life, she says.

# my father's regrets

My father and I snag a table in the hospital lunchroom.

Upstairs, my mother struggles with one thing after another, all of which started, she claims, because she foolishly tripped on her shoelace and fell against the coffee table in the living room while turning off the lights in preparation for bed. Impossible, says my Sherlockian brother David. At that point in the evening *she would not have been wearing her shoes.* Okay, she admits, she'd secretly been having dizzy spells for months—but she is adamant that they had nothing whatsoever to do with her fall, she is just a terrible *klutz.*

My father heard a crash, found her on the floor, and somehow grappled her into the bedroom. Only in the morning did they call anyone—my sister Becky, who was understandably furious that they hadn't called an ambulance right away. "You shouldn't have moved her!" she yelled at my father. "Don't you know anything?" She hung up and made another call, and instantly, it seemed, EMTs were swarming all over the apartment. My mother was mortified.

At the hospital, they X-rayed her and sent her home. They noticed her cracked pelvis only in the second set of X-rays, after she'd been immobilized and in terrible pain for a week—it must have been terrible, because otherwise my mother would never have mentioned it. When she was finally admitted, her blood pressure was careening up and down, and her heart was beating wildly; her legs had swelled up, and she coughed every time she tried to draw a breath. Now, she has an internist, a cardiologist, a pulmonologist, an orthopedist, physical therapists, nurses—but somehow none of them are ever around when a crisis happens or even when she has a question or wants to try walking down the corridor, which they've forbidden her to do without a professional to supervise. We in the family don't qualify, and that's that.

Every new remedy creates another frightening problem: the blood thinners make her faint; the blood pressure regulators make her readings even more erratic; the pain killers don't kill the pain, and then when they do, they confuse and constipate her; the diuretics make her lose control of her bladder and bowels; the diaper is simply humiliating. She's exhausted but she can't sleep. She's emaciated but food appalls her. They tell her she'll have to stay on oxygen for the rest of her life, tethered to a big green tank that will clear the way for her wherever she goes, causing people to look away or to stare, bellowing, I'M A SICK OLD LADY.

If she has a rest-of-her-life. It doesn't look good.

"I don't want to live like that, anyway."

"Oh, Ma," we say. "Please don't say that. You'll get used to it. They have portable ones."

She doesn't answer.

The lunchroom has round wooden tables, each set with a cut-glass vase holding two carnations, knobby captain's chairs, and frilly curtains. It's staffed by volunteers—teenage girls, elderly ladies, and a few extremely geeky boys in their twenties. The arrangement must have seemed like a good idea at the time, but the volunteers, though friendly, are incompetent. They're always running out of basics like sandwich bread, and my father is the world's most impatient customer. Today, several of them in succession stop by the table to apologize because the dishwasher is broken and they're serving on plastic.

None of them takes our order. My father looks as though he's about to explode. They aren't sure about the soup of the day but they'll check.

"I've had a good life," he says, when we're finally served our tuna sandwiches. "I could go any time." He often tells me this, as does my mother, who adds, "At our age we don't even buy green bananas." It's a cliché, but because I'm not in my eighties I've never heard it before and think it's clever. Today my father continues, "I have three regrets."

"Only three?" I say, for a little joke.

He ignores me and ticks them off on his fingers: "I'll never forgive myself for slapping Priscilla. I lost the Pepsi account. And I should have been home more when you kids were growing up."

## Regret #1: Slapping Priscilla.   I wonder if Priscilla even remembers. That's the way it is with regrets. You beat yourself up for fifty years and to the other person it's like it never happened. (So, did it?)

I don't bring this up, but I have the same feeling about Judy—the one and only person I've ever physically attacked in my life. I was maybe sixteen, so she would have been around twelve, and we were in the cottage in Great Barrington. For a change, no one else was around. The age difference between Judy and me is small enough so that it drove me crazy, as a teenager, to watch her going through the same miseries I just had. Yet even if she had been willing to listen to my advice, some things are not explicable. People just have to experience them for themselves.

She had said some typically annoying thing, and I couldn't stand it anymore and starting pounding her on the shoulders, which were at the level of my still new and hated breasts. It was an odd thing to do, and the feeling of it has stayed with me. She just stood there, taking it. Among us kids we generally stuck to verbal abuse, so neither of us was an experienced fighter.

(Years later, when I worked at the homeless shelter, an angry woman no one had ever seen before came in for lunch. She was shouting at everyone and making a lot of noise, so I went over to see what was going on. She continued shouting, now at me, crowding me closer and closer, until she was right up in my face. Then she turned over a table and left. The women gathered around me. They had been frightened for me, they said. Hadn't I understood that she was trying to provoke me to take a swing at her so she could knock me down in self-defense? I had not. Hitting hadn't occurred to me, either as something that she would do or that I would. It just isn't in my physical repertoire.)

Priscilla was wild, at least in comparison to the rest of us. She kissed boys in cars, she hung out with her girlfriends all afternoon playing foosball in the basement instead of going to school, she shoplifted makeup and smoked cigarettes and got bad grades. She stayed out until all hours and then came home without her coat. How do you lose an expensive winter coat? Don't you notice that it's cold outside? The thing about Priscilla, though, was that she always got caught, even for things no one ever gets caught for—asking a creepy guy outside the liquor store to buy her a six pack, illegal parking, fake ID, smoking in the girls' room, clipping math class and going out for lunch. There were constant calls from cops, teachers, the principal, her friends' parents, Woolworth's security guards, waitresses. She had no secrets.

"I was at a loss," says my father. I was in college during Priscilla's high school years, so I missed all the drama. I don't know what finally pushed him over the edge, and he doesn't say. "But look how she's turned out," he adds. As an adult, Priscilla is funny, kind, loving, insightful, and law-abiding. Her husband and her three kids adore her. She gets along with everyone. No one would ever want to slap her.

Regret #2: Lost Pepsi Account.   My father is a sales-
man, flavors and colors—in college I told this to someone who
mused, "How abstract." But flavors and colors aren't abstract
at all; each taste or smell has its own chemical formula, my
father says.

When I was growing up, the trunk of his car was always full
of samples, and we kids hated riding in it. The smell was over-
powering; it immediately made us nauseous. "Oh, for chrissake,"
my father swore. Whenever he traveled by plane, he would grab
a couple of airsick bags from the seat pocket to keep in his glove
compartment. He claimed the car had no unusual smell, and he
didn't know what we were complaining about. And if it did, so
what? It was his livelihood and we should be grateful.

He'd started out as a chemist, working in the General Foods
lab in Hoboken, New Jersey. On his lunch breaks, he could
take a stroll and watch the filming of *On the Waterfront*. His
team was developing cake mixes. Most people don't realize it,
he says, but it would be possible to manufacture a cake mix
for which all you'd have to do is add water and presto! instant
cake—but the product wouldn't sell. The housewives like to
feel they're creating something. So you leave out the eggs, the
milk—things for them to do.

His division was relocated to Tarrytown, New York, and my
parents considered moving there. I have an early memory of an
afternoon of excruciating boredom spent looking at half-built
houses surrounded by fields of mud. Perhaps I was wearing an
adorable blue snowsuit with little animal ears on the hood, as
in one of my parents' home movies. I hope so, although I have
another early memory of throwing a tantrum, flinging my arms
and legs about as my mother tried to bundle me into my snowsuit. We stayed in New Jersey, and my father went into sales.

It's been a great career for him. He likes meeting people. He
immediately discerns their good qualities—their intelligence,
their unusual talents, their interesting life stories. My father

is an admirer. As he tells it, he's been surrounded all his life by remarkable characters. He's also a loyalist. He would bring home product prototypes for us to try: chocolate pudding in a can, which was better than it sounds; instant spaghetti in a plastic bag. Then there was lecithin powder, to sprinkle on top of oatmeal in the morning. It didn't improve the taste, but my father believed it was very healthy, and he gave big jars of it to all of his friends and acquaintances. Occasionally he still mentions it: he has various crank theories about cholesterol and the body's infection-fighting mechanisms. They don't involve a low-fat diet, but they do involve lecithin. His cardiologist doesn't want to hear a word of it, even when my father offers to take him out to dinner so they can discuss it in detail, on my father's dime. "The guy refused my invitation!" my father says. "All he wants to do is give out pills."

My father's sales territory was the whole Northeast, so he did a lot of driving in his smelly car, up to Boston, out to Albany. Soap operas were on the radio in those days, and he knew all the plots. When my parents' friends came to visit, he could discuss them with the wives. In the ashtray he kept a roll or two of peppermint Life Savers, which he would occasionally share with us, but as candies they were a big disappointment, so strong you had to spit them out.

As for the Pepsi account—somehow I had assumed that caffeine occurs naturally in Pepsi, which is absurd if you think about it, that anything about Pepsi occurs naturally. They used to buy the stuff by the truckload from my father, until they discovered they could get it cheaper in China. It was a big loss for his company, and it put the guys on the caffeine assembly line out of work. He blames himself, but it's obviously a bigger phenomenon.

## Regret #3: Should Have Been Home More When You Kids Were Growing Up.

There was a period in my twenties when everyone I met revealed some awful type of family dysfunction—beatings, addictions, unholy sexual appetites, bankruptcies—and I began searching for signs of it in my own sane life. I would sometimes claim that I'd had an absent father. It's true, he did a lot of traveling, but then, I have certain memories: my mother taught us all to swim, but my father taught me to ride a bicycle, running back and forth beside me on the sidewalk, pushing and letting go until suddenly I got it, the balance, it was simple, falling off became the trick. Errands with a gaggle of kids didn't faze him: he would drag us to the Lower East Side for cheap eyeglasses and once on the ferry to the Statue of Liberty, where he took a snapshot of us lined up in size order, me towering over my brothers and sisters, with my hair in long braids. My mother took us to the regular dentist—whose waiting room was full of comic books, which we were not allowed to have at home—but it was my father who took me to the orthodontist to have braces put on. Walking home, we ran into a friend of his, and they stopped on the sidewalk and had a long conversation while I stood there, aware only of my teeth. Finally, he pointed me out. "The thousand-dollar smile," he said. I covered my mouth with my hand.

At the moment when he and I could have drawn closest, I pulled away, but not on purpose. In the summer of my junior year of high school, I went to Israel, on a tour sponsored by a Jewish youth group. My father had dreamed of going to Israel all his life, and now I would be the family emissary. That June I went to Great Barrington as usual, but just for a few weeks. On the Sunday of the week I was scheduled to leave, my father and I drove back to New Jersey together.

Packing for Israel was very difficult. Most of the room in my suitcase was taken up by a box of sanitary napkins—I didn't know how to request them in Hebrew and absolutely did not intend to learn—and several wrapped presents that my grand-parents had instructed me to deliver with their compliments to some non-English-speaking Madorskys who lived outside of Haifa. They said I should call their relatives on the telephone when I arrived and arrange to spend my free weekends on their kibbutz. Since my grandparents had traveled from Russia to Detroit with no English and about fifty cents in their pockets, the logistical and communication problems to which this errand would subject me probably didn't seem like much to them, but to me they seemed insurmountable.

When I wasn't packing, I spent the days before my trip listening to records and reading poetry by Rod McKuen with Rosemary Kucinski, a tall, charismatic girl with whom I'd become friends only the previous spring. "Oh, don't go to Israel," she said. "Stay here with me. Wouldn't it be fun?"

"Daddy," I said in desperation, on the morning I was scheduled to leave. "Couldn't I stay in Rutherford at Rosemary's house for the summer? We could get the money for Israel back. I haven't gotten on the plane yet."

"For chrissake," said my father. "You're going." We drove to Newark Airport in silence.

Once I got to Israel, the other girls showed me how to use tampons, and when after a perfunctory try I couldn't figure out how to work the Israeli payphone, I ditched the presents without even opening them to see what they were.

I dismissed the notion of an absent father a long time ago, so it surprises me when he lists this as a regret. Apparently I didn't completely fabricate the idea. Judy and my mother and I were reminiscing recently about something or other, and my father said, "I don't remember that," and Judy said, I think more harshly than she'd intended, "Of course you don't. You were never around." I could see it stung him.

Paying the bill in the hospital cafeteria, my father says, "I hope your mother recovers in time for us to go to Florida." They go every winter and stay for six weeks.

"I hope so too, Daddy," I say, although at that moment recovery seems like a dream, my mother has become so fragile. I had confided in Becky, "I think she has congestive heart failure," and Becky had nodded.

But amazingly, my mother does recover. Her pneumonia clears up, and her blood pressure stabilizes, and the doctors want her to go to rehab to build up her strength—which infuriates her. "I want to go back to my normal routine," she says. "I want to get out of here."

I'm grateful to see her old stubbornness showing itself, but I tell her I agree with the doctors. She's not ready yet for the apartment. She can't even get out of bed without help; how would my father take care of her? He thinks he can, but we all work to dissuade him, and finally he gives in. At least they both agree that driving to Florida is out of the question. The trip is too long and exhausting, and they'd be too far from help.

It's too bad, though. It would be so comforting to think of them there, well and happy, my mother swimming in the motel pool, my father playing golf. In Florida they read, they walk the bridge over the Intracoastal Waterway each morning, they visit their friends. The weather is mild and breezy. When my father calls me on Saturday mornings he says, "It's seventy-five degrees here!"

"Here it's twenty!" I yell. His hearing aid doesn't seem to work over the telephone. "And snowing!" He couldn't be more pleased. "I'm going to spend the afternoon shoveling the driveway!" I add, to make him feel even better.

In Florida, my mother doesn't have to cook a thing. The motel provides breakfast, my parents hide a few extra yogurts and some fruit in their pockets for lunch, and for dinner they go to the early birds with the other *alte kockers*. Since they've been making this trip to Florida every year, my brothers think my parents should buy a condominium. It would be much nicer than the motel, and a good investment, too. "But that would ruin everything!" says my mother. "I'd have to shop, I'd have to clean."

"Why do you always come back so early?" I harangue my father every year. They leave Florida in early March, when New Jersey is cold and dark, and the sidewalks are too icy for them to take their morning walk. "You'll just be stuck indoors. You can afford to stay away a little longer."

"I feel guilty," he says, although I've never thought of him as the guilt-ridden type. That's me and my mother.

"That's insane."

He smiles and shrugs. In his mid-eighties, he's still working. "I have to make a few sales calls," he says.

"But you could do that from Palm Beach!"

"I could," he says. "But your mother and I want to go home."

# the wedding

A few years ago—I never remember how many exactly, but I know it was Thanksgiving weekend—Roberta and I got married: because we live in Massachusetts, because it was there, so to speak. I don't want to be too cynical, because the wedding itself was a kind of event I'd wanted to plan for a long time—family and dear friends, or rather, straight family and gay family, all gathered into the same room and introduced to one another. We held it in crazy, beautiful Provincetown. Everyone went home with a story to tell. A gay man stopped my mother on the street and exclaimed, "Sweetheart, I *love* your coat!" which made her happy all weekend, since the fuzzy electric-blue plaid had been a terrific bargain at Loehmann's. My father mistook Ellie— the miniskirted cross-dresser who croons Frank Sinatra songs in front of Town Hall, her sign propped on her amplifier, "78 Years Young: Living My Dream"—for a woman. Enlightened, he said, "Not a bad voice." And since that weekend, whenever I see my brother David, he goes on and on about the Christmas tableau in the window of the sex-toy shop, a mechanical Santa whipping an elf. He claims it was his daughters who were trau- matized by the Santa, but they were children. They've forgotten all about it.

Although I don't remember the date of my wedding, my mother does, and she calls yearly to wish me and Roberta a happy anniversary. The first time she may even have sent a

card—and we are not a card-sending family. Like most lesbians, though, Roberta and I have always counted our anniversary from the first time we had sex, a date celebrated by us but
not my mother.

Our decision to get married was the result of a misunder-
standing, at least on my part. I thought it was Roberta who
was pushing to do it, while she seems to think it was me, when
I was only following what I thought was her lead. She's the
one in our relationship who deals with bills, property, money,
while I regularly screw up the arithmetic in our checkbook. I
thought she wanted to get married because of what seemed
to me an irrational obsession about the taxes an unmarried
survivor would apparently have to pay on our apartment if
one of us died, because she is convinced she will go first. My
parents are still alive, while hers died years ago of heritable
diseases. Knowing my financial incompetence, she wanted to
protect me; but it was exactly that financial incompetence that
made it impossible for me to imagine such taxes would apply
to me in that awful situation, and in any case how can you plan
for something so completely beyond anyone's control. Roberta
says we made the decision to marry mutually, for political rea-
sons, to support our progressive Commonwealth, to plant our
rainbow flag.

So here we are, for better and for worse. It hasn't made much
difference in our relationship—we'd already been together for
sixteen years by the time of the wedding. It does create certain
annoying and tedious tax complications due to the irrational
U.S. healthcare system and differences in the federal and state
understandings of our relationship—a novelty, since before
the wedding, the government had no interest in our relationship one way or the other. I've never yet managed to refer in
casual conversation to Roberta as "my wife." I am a women's
liberationist who came up in the 1970s, when we had slogans
like "Rape is the theory; marriage is the practice," and "No

nukes"—meaning both bombs and families. We believed marriage was irredeemable, a patriarchal structure that enslaved us and our kids, a microcosm of sexist oppression. When homophobes shouted at my gay male comrades, "Which one of you is the wife?" they blew kisses and shrieked back, "We *both* are!" Of course neither Roberta nor I is the wife, and I still can't figure out how our movement devolved into this one issue, of gay marriage—although we doubled brides and grooms do, quite satisfyingly, freak a lot of people out. I'm freaked out myself. It sounds bizarre to me to hear a lesbian refer to her wife. I call Roberta my lover, my girlfriend, or, around straight people, my partner—although then they think we're in business together, and in fact just last week a new colleague of Roberta's asked her, "Oh, so you and Amy sell real estate?"

"My *life* partner," Roberta had to explain. "Amy" doesn't even belong in the same sentence as "sell real estate."

I meet straight girls in the gym who chatter all the time about their "husbands," so what's my problem? "Wife" would simply be parallel, but I can't bring myself to throw it into the conversation. As for gay men and "husband": my friend Will, in San Francisco, whose linguistic mannerisms have always been totally contagious, uses the word to mean something like "trick." "I'm off to find a *husband*," he'll say, getting on his bicycle to pedal over to a certain section of Golden Gate Park, so he'll get a little exercise in the process.

When Roberta and I announced our intention to get married, we discovered how much the world loves a wedding. Being gay, we'd never fully experienced the extent of it. The attraction is so strong that even homophobes can't help loving our weddings. I swear I once heard a National Public Radio reporter ask Mitt Romney whether, if he were invited to the wedding of two gay friends, he would attend. After a bit of hesitation, he said yes. And he sounded unusually sincere, as though he would have looked forward to such an occasion, and as though he were wishing that he had gay friends. When we sent out the invitations, I thought a lot of people would turn us down—after all, my family and friends are busy people, and I wasn't convinced they'd all endorse the idea. But everyone responded immediately that they'd love to come, as though they'd been waiting for just this moment for years—and maybe they had been. At work I was presented with a basket decorated with a white ribbon containing a bottle of champagne and a pair of glasses. We would never have gotten the gift for a commitment ceremony. Even now, some number of years later, when I tell people Roberta and I are married, they get all dreamy-eyed. Awww. They demand to see photos, which Roberta has helpfully posted on her website.

We went with a Unitarian minister because she said we could write our own vows, while the other officiants we'd interviewed explained that although they could offer an array of ceremonies—the civil, the beach, the Native American—whatever we did had to fit one of their formats. Our minister just asked hesitantly whether it would be okay if she wore her robe and stole. "We do our thing; you do yours," we said. When she pronounced the formula—"In accordance with the laws of the Commonwealth of Massachusetts, you are now married"—everyone applauded and cheered, and our friend Kate showed off her skill at whistling through her teeth. My mother, of all people, rose to make a toast. There was no longer any doubt: I was back in the bosom of my family.

# my father goes down to hell

On Yom Kippur my mother says she wants to go to the *yizkor* service, but my father says he has no need of it, not because he is an unbeliever, which he is, but because even at his age not a day goes by when he doesn't think of his parents. He doesn't need to go to a special service to remember them.

My parents now attend my sister Priscilla's temple for the high holidays, because of a falling out at their former *shul.* "That rabbi was a nut," my father says. "A right-winger." The rabbi had put up a *mechitzah,* a curtain of separation between the men and the women, decorated along the top with plastic flowers. The first year it appeared, my father mocked it. "Rabbi," he called out. "I have a complaint! The *mechitzah* is too low. I can look over it and see my wife. She will distract me from my prayers!"

The next fall, when it showed up again, he objected in earnest. "The family!" he instructed the rabbi. "This is the basis of Jewish observance. I want to sit in *shul* with my wife and children." He narrowed his eyes. "In Auschwitz," he said, "the Nazis sent the men in one direction and the women in another."

"Oh, Sig," said my mother.

"Maybe you don't belong in this congregation anymore," said the rabbi.

"What!" cried my father. "The memorial plaques for my parents are in the sanctuary!" Little orange bulbs flicker on their *yahrzeits,* the anniversaries of their deaths. "They are buried in the Temple Beth-El cemetery plot!" None of us has ever visited them there—what's the point? Dead is dead. But it's reassuring to know where they are: right off Route 3, overlooking the former drive-in movie theater. "I belong in this temple, Rabbi. I donated my father's Yiddish books to the library. His Yiddish Talmud. Where are his books?"

The rabbi shrugged.

My father returned to the temple one Sunday to rescue his father's books and intruded on a Bible study class. The men were discussing the binding of Isaac. Our father Abraham, one offered, was a model of faith and courage for the generations in his willingness to sacrifice his son at God's whim.

"You're barbarians!" my father exclaimed.

The library, it turned out, had been dismantled, and the books thrown with indifference into the basement, in giant plastic bags. My father didn't have the strength to lift or sort them, and no one from upstairs offered to help. They're ruined, but he still aims to go back. The appointments never work out.

My father says his father would look in the mirror and ask himself, "How did I get to be so old?" He told my father, "Life is an *oygnblik*"—the blink of an eye.

Now, my father says, he asks himself the same question: Who is that old man? Although what exactly my father sees is a mystery—and not only because his Coke-bottle glasses don't entirely correct his vision.

"Amazing how my hair is still so black," he muses, glancing at himself in the hallway mirror.

My mother and I laugh at him. She has always had wonderful hair, naturally wavy, and it went gray with a Sontagian streak down the middle. Now it's bright white. I so hope mine will do the same, but it will probably be more like my father's. Steely and growing straight down over my small forehead.

"Are you kidding?" my mother says to my father. "You've been gray for years. Like me."

"Nah."

His poor vision frustrates him—unlike his poor hearing, which he seems to enjoy. It frees him from the obligation to follow the conversations of others. David says, "This is Siggy and Aunt Norma." He looks to his right: "What? I can't hear you! Stop mumbling!" He looks to his left: "What? I can't hear you! Stop mumbling!"

My father hates to wear his hearing aids. They're uncomfortable, no good. "What do you expect from Ears-R-Us," Becky tells him. "Get some decent ones."

"Nope," he says. "Too noisy."

My grandmother's vision became so distorted she couldn't focus on the Yiddish newspaper, even before the Alzheimer's. My grandfather read to her. Now, doesn't this suggest a peaceful scene, both of them in rockers? That was not their relationship. She would mock his accent, his low voice. "Speak up!" she would yell.

My father, a scientist, interested in the latest technology, wants laser eye surgery. Priscilla had it, and she woke up the next morning and threw away her glasses, like she'd been to Lourdes. But my father's eye doctor says he's too old, my father tells me. Eventually he'll need cataract surgery, the doctor says, and maybe that will correct his vision.

"So, that's the story, sweetheart," my father concludes. "When I go I'll see perfectly. The flames, the flames coming toward me!"

# at the lake #2

When I tell people I learned to swim in Lake Erie, they look at me funny. But that was back in 1959. I was seven and consented to submerge myself only because my brother David, two years younger, had done it first, humiliating me. By the late 1960s, the idea of a family vacation there had become ludicrous. Erie had by then become famous not for its sandy beaches and warm, shallow water but for being a toxic sea of industrial effluvia and sewage, with a polluted Dead Zone in the middle and the flaming Cuyahoga River emptying into it at Cleveland. We went to Lake Erie only that one summer; afterward, it was the Berkshires and Lake Buel every year.

Our cottage was on the eastern shore of the lake, which in our opinion was far superior to the west. For one thing, our side of the lake got the afternoon sun. We could swim and play at the dock until the magic hour of 5:00, when the breezes calmed, the motorboats returned to their slips, and the water stilled. The reflection of the mountains, which had broken up a few hours after dawn, reappeared. "The best time of the day!" my parents said, when we complained that we were bored and hungry. "We can't leave now!" We'd appreciate it for another half hour or so, then climb back up the hill to the cottage, where my mother would begin dinner. Sometimes, after the meal, we'd return to watch the sun go down.

On the other side of the lake, the water was mucky and the

bottom full of weeds so high they poked their heads above the surface. Some areas were blanketed with water lilies. The white ones with yellow centers were beautiful, until you leaned out of the canoe to pick one and discovered it was crawling with bugs and, with reflexive disgust, flung it out of the boat. The yellow ones were simply grotesque, looking a little like bugs themselves, or at least parts of bugs—antennae waving in the air. In contrast, in our swimming area the water was so clear you could see through it all the way down to your feet shimmering on the hard, rocky bottom. Tiny sunfish would gather while you stood there contemplating your dive into the chilly water, to nip at your calves.

Not any more. In an inexorable natural cycle, our lake is turning into a swamp, which will one day become a meadow, and finally the spongy surface of the forest. Now it's not only the western shore that's afflicted with lake weed and muck; even around our dock, the weeds are high, the water green and opaque with algae, the bottom squishy between your toes. Each spring a guy hired by the Lake Buel Association drives around and around in a weed-cutting barge, and sitting on the dock, we beckon to him: Come in closer! Closer, damn it! You're not accomplishing anything out there in the middle of the lake! But he's cautious of ruining his spinning blades on the rocks. In any case, this solution is only temporary; the weeds grow and grow, and he has to be called back again and again. Rumor has it that a lady up in Stockbridge proposed solving her pond eutrophication problem by dumping Agent Orange into the water. There was an outcry, and she backed off, supposedly. This summer my father notices with approval that that the weeds in Lake Buel are not nearly as widespread or persistent as usual. Maybe they just gave up, after all those years of attack. There's no smell, no tint to the water that I can discern, but the fish, my father notices, are also gone. The fishermen drift by in their rowboats in the late afternoon, and when we yell,

Catch anything? instead of waving a trout, they shake their heads. Nah. Nice day, though.

Up at the cottage, our water comes from a well. When I was a child, my mother would pour me a cup. According to her, like our beautiful lake water, it was a *mechiah*, fresh and sweet. According to me, it was water. And the love of my family, in which I swam like a little sunfish, was as boring and tasteless as a glass of water from the faucet. It's not like we're in the desert, Ma.

A child's view. Of course we are, unless we're lucky.

# acknowledgments

It's a pleasure to acknowledge the many people who helped me take the journey of writing this book. My parents, Sigmund and Serena Hoffman, have loved and supported me all my life both unconditionally and for my accomplishments, and continue to inspire me every day with their humanistic values, warmth, curiosity, and intelligence. They, and my Aunt Norma Salz, put up with many hours of interrogation by me and requests to dig around in old photo albums and other artifacts. My brothers and sisters, David Hoffman, Judith Hoffman, Priscilla Morrissey, Rebecca Hoffman, and Joshua Hoffman, have paid me the compliment of reading this manuscript, jogging my memory, and challenging me. As my mother reminds us, every sibling grows up in a different family. I especially thank Priscilla for her ever-dependable wisdom, humor, and grace.

As always, I am grateful to my dear longtime writing buddies, Anita Diamant and Stephen McCauley, without whose encouragement, friendship, and willingness to read and critique innumerable iterations of a manuscript I would never have had the confidence to finish this book or any other.

Cookie Avrin, Richard Burns, Kate Clinton, Betsy Smith, Roberta Stone, and Urvashi Vaid read and discussed with me early versions of this book—as well as sharing dinners, conversations, political debates, dune walks, hikes, bicycle adventures, and celebrations for the past thirty-whatever years. We'll keep each other going for another thirty, dolls.

My colleagues at the Wellesley Centers for Women—especially the third-floor lunch crew—have made our office much more than a workplace. They're friends, sources of ideas and insight, and even proofreaders (thanks, Ineke Ceder). Meg Kearney and Tanya Whiton at the Solstice Low-Residency MFA Program at Pine Manor College have encouraged my teaching, given me opportunities to try out new work on unsuspecting audiences, and generally made me feel like a real writer. For making me feel like a real writer I also thank Mary Cappello, who in addition to being a great cook has organized readings and taught my books in her courses at the University of Rhode Island. Because of her kind recommendation, my book chapter "My Grandmother Was Sent Forth" was published in the *Ocean State Review* in June 2012.

A literary friend once advised me, "Writing the book is the best part"—but Brian Halley, my editor at the University of Massachusetts Press, and his colleagues Bruce Wilcox, Carol Betsch, and Sally Nichols, have made publication and promotion anxiety-free and even fun.

A generous fellowship at the gorgeous Virginia Center for the Creative Arts enabled me to give my book manuscript a final, much-needed going-over.

For twenty-five years, Roberta Stone has been not only a loving and literarily astute life partner—and a good speller—but also the coolest person I know.

AMY HOFFMAN is the author of two award-winning memoirs, *Hospital Time* (1997), about taking care of friends with AIDS in the late 1990s, and *An Army of Ex-Lovers: My Life at the "Gay Community News"* (2007). She is editor in chief of *Women's Review of Books* and a faculty member at the Solstice Low-Residency MFA Program at Pine Manor College. Hoffman has a BA from Brandeis University and an MFA from the University of Massachusetts Amherst. Born in New Jersey, she lives in Jamaica Plain, Massachusetts, with her wife, Roberta Stone.

54⁰⁰ Den 5/16 K